ORGANIZATIONS IN ACTION

Classics in Organization and Management
Robert T. Golembiewski, series editor

The Anatomy of Work, Georges Friedman

Approaches to Planned Change, Robert T. Golembiewski

The Changing of Organizational Behavior Patterns, Paul R. Lawrence

Executive Talent, Eli Ginzberg, editor

Integrating the Individual and the Organization, Chris Argyris

Ironies in Organizational Development, Robert T. Golembiewski

The Limits of Organizational Change, Herbert Kaufman

Managing Large Systems, Leonard R. Sayles and Margaret K. Chandler

Men, Management, and Morality, Robert T. Golembiewski

The Motivation to Work, Frederick Herzberg, Bernard Mausner, and Barbara Snyderman

Motives and Goals in Groups, Alvin Zander

New Forms of Work Organization in Europe, Peter Grootings, Bjorn Gustavson, and Lajos Héthy, editors

The New Society, Peter F. Drucker

Organization Development, Robert T. Golembiewski

Organizations in Action, James D. Thompson

Public Administration, Herbert A. Simon, Donald W. Smithburg, and Victor A. Thompson

The Rise of the Meritocracy, Michael Young

ORGANIZATIONS IN ACTION

Social Science Bases of Administrative Theory

James D. Thompson

with a new preface by
Mayer N. Zald

and a new introduction by
W. Richard Scott

Transaction Publishers
New Brunswick (U.S.A.) and London (U.K.)

Sixth printing 2008

New material this edition copyright © 2003 by Transaction Publishers, New Brunswick, New Jersey. Originally published in 1967 by McGraw-Hill Book Company.

This book is printed on acid-free paper that meets the American National Standard for Permanence of Paper for Printed Library Materials.

Library of Congress Catalog Number: 2002027185
ISBN: 978-0-7658-0991-9
Printed in the United States of America

Library of Congress Cataloging-in-Publication Data

Thompson, James D.
    Organizations in action : social science bases of administrative theory / James D. Thompson ; with a new preface by Mayer N. Zald and a new introduction by W. Richard Scott.
        p. cm.-(Classics   in organization and management)
    Originally published: New York : McGraw-Hill, 1967. With new preface and introd.
        Includes bibliographical references and index.
        ISBN 0-7658-0991-5 (pbk. : alk. paper)
        1. Industrial organization. I. Title. II. Classics in organization and management series.

HD31 .T4888 2003
302.3'5—dc21   2002027185

to my families and shay

contents

preface to the transaction edition

Jim Thompson published *Organizations in Action* in 1967. It was widely acclaimed and quickly established itself as a modern classic, widely cited and used. It served not only as a stimulating theory that guided and provoked ideas for research, but also as a textbook. A generation of students in business schools and sociology departments read it and were thus introduced to the frontiers of the sociological analysis of organizations. Although he did not use the term, Thompson can be thought of as one of the founding fathers of contingency theory. In contrast to an earlier approach to administrative theory, which focused upon the "one best way" and upon universal generalizations about organizations, Thompson emphasized that organizational structure and dynamics was heavily dependent upon the imperatives of technology, goals, environmental pressures, and problems of coordination. The different shapes of organizational structures and organizational responses were heavily contingent upon differences in technology, coordination problems, and environmental pressures that were found in different industries.

By the time *Organizations in Action* was published, Thompson had already established himself as one of the foremost students of organizations of his generation. A master of the incisive essay, his métier was the careful use of important conceptual distinctions to show how the variety of organizational forms, from collegial groups to bureaucracies, from cults to legislative bodies, could be seen as human creations to solve a variety of decision making and coordination problems. He showed how organizational goals were established in a kind of interactive process as organizations responded to environmental conditions. From the analysis of organizational and administrative responses to disasters, to the analysis of the relationship of administration to societal development, his deep sociological insight illuminated the meso-processes of social organization. *Organizations in Action* only solidified his reputation for a distinctive voice of great acuity and clarity. He did this in a very short time span.

Thompson was born on January 11, 1920 in Indianapolis, Indiana.[1] In 1932 he moved to Chicago, where his father was employed by Standard Oil. He graduated from public high school in Chicago, and then went to Indiana University, where he obtained a B.A. degree in business, with an emphasis upon financial writing. He entered the Air Force before Pearl Harbor in 1941 and served until 1946. Obtaining a master's degree in journalism, he took a job as an editor with the Chicago Journal of Commerce for six months and then taught journalism at the University of Wisconsin. Thompson entered the doctoral program in sociology at the University of North Carolina, Chapel Hill in 1950, receiving his Ph.D. in 1954. (He had actually wanted a doctorate in communications, but at that time could not find an appropriate degree program.)

Following his stay at Chapel Hill, he took a job in the School of Business and Public Administration at Cornell. Edward Litchfield, a charismatic and dynamic administrator/intellectual, was then dean, and Thompson and Litchfield made common cause. Together they founded the *Administrative Science Quarterly*, with Thompson as first editor. (*ASQ* has been the preeminent, or one of the preeminent, scholarly journals in the field of organizational studies for more than forty years.) When Litchfield took a position as chancellor of the University of Pittsburgh Thompson followed, becoming the director of the newly created Administrative Science Center there in 1957. In 1962 he moved back to Indiana University, holding a joint appointment in the School of Business and the Department of Sociology. In 1968 he joined the faculty of the Department of Sociology at Vanderbilt, where we met and became friends. Four years later he was diagnosed with cancer. He died on September 1, 1973 at the age of fifty-four. (My youngest son's middle name is James, in his honor.)

Organizations in Action was published in 1967. Although Thompson published several more theoretical essays and empirical studies after that, many of his later publications moved away from the study of organizations per se. By himself, and with others, he wrote on the family life cycle, on societal development, and on the role of public administration in societal development. (A list of all of his publications is included at the end of this Preface.) Although Jim's essays remain cogent and stand up well over time,[2] *Organizations in Action* is the summa of his thinking, the most extensive and comprehensive working out of his comparative analysis of the dynamics of organizations.

It was part of the standard reading of advanced students of administration and management for twenty years. It went out of print more than a decade ago, yet it continues to be cited and used, even though contingency theory and the comparative approach that informed his style of thinking is no longer as prominent as it once was. Many of Thompson's insights and chapters can be seen as forerunners of later theoretical developments. Since so many scholars continue to use it, often distributing copies of chapters to their classes, I am delighted that Transaction Publishers has agreed to reprint it. I am also delighted that W. Richard Scott, one of the leading sociologists of his generation and *the* leading analyst of the history and transformation of the sociological study of organizations, has written the introduction to this reprinting. It is an elegant and incisive presentation of the place of Thompson's classic in the study of organizations.

mayer n. zald
university of michigan

NOTES

1. I am indebted to Mary Thompson for providing me with information about Jim Thompson's life.
2. William Rushing and I edited a collection of his essays, *Organizations and Beyond: Selected Essays of James D. Thompson* (Lexington, MA: D.C. Heath-Lexington Books, 1976).

COMPLETE BIBLIOGRAPHY OF JAMES D. THOMPSON

"Community Patterns of Idea Intake," in *Journalism Quarterly*, Winter, 1951, pp. 49-57.

With N. J. Dermerath, "Some Experiences with the Group Interview," in *Social Forces*, vol. 31, December, 1952, pp. 148-154.

"On Building an Administrative Science," *Administrative Science Quarterly*, vol. 1, June, 1956, pp. 102-111.

"Authority and Power in 'Identical' Organizations," *American Journal of Sociology*, vol. 62, November, 1956, pp. 290-301.

With F. L. Bates, "Technology, Organization and Administration," *Administrative Science Quarterly*, vol. 2, December, 1957, pp. 325-343.

"Modern Approaches to Theory in Administration," in Andrew Halpin, ed., *Administrative Theory in Education* (Midwest Administration Center, University of Chicago, 1958).

With William J. McEwen, "Organizational Goals and Environment: Goal-Setting as an Interaction Process," *American Sociological Review*, vol. 23, February, 1958, pp. 23-31.

Co-editor, *Comparative Studies in Administration* (University of Pittsburgh Press, 1959).

"Organizational Management of Conflict," in *Administrative Science Quarterly*, vol. 4, March, 1960, pp. 389-409.

"Common Elements in Administration," chapter in Ella W. Reed, ed., *Social Welfare Administration* (New York: Columbia University Press, 1961).

With Arthur Tuden, "Organizational Decision-Making," *Series Research in Social Psychology*, Symposia Studies Series, National Institute of Social Behavioral Science, Fall, 1961.

With Robert W. Hawkes, "Disaster, Community Organization, and Administrative Process," chapter in George W. Baker and Dwight W. Chapman, eds., *Man and Society in Disaster* (New York: Basic Books, 1962), pp. 268-300.

"Common and Uncommon Elements in Administration," chapter in *The Social Welfare Forum*, 1962, Official Proceedings of the National Conference on Social Welfare (New York: Columbia University Press, 1962).

"Organizations and Output Transactions," *American Journal of Sociology*, November, 1962, pp. 309-324.

"A Rationale for Viewing Organizational Conflict," chapter in Jack Culbertson and Stephen Hencley, eds., *Educational Research: New Perspectives* (Danville, Illinois: The Interstate Printers and Publishers, 1963).

"How to Prevent Innovations," *Trans-Action*, vol. 2, January/February, 1965, p. 30.

Editor, *Approaches to Organizational Design* (Pittsburgh: University of Pittsburgh Press, 1966).

Organizations in Action (New York: McGraw-Hill, 1967).

With Richard O. Carlson and Robert W. Avery, "Occupations, Personnel and Careers," *Educational Administration Quarterly*, Winter, 1968, pp. 6-31.

"Models of Organization and Administrative Systems," in *The Social Sciences: Problems and Orientations* (The Hague: Mouton/Unesco, 1968).

With Robert W. Avery and Robert W. Hawkes, "Truth Strategies and University Organization," *Educational Administration Quarterly*, Spring, 1969.

With Donald R. Van Houten, *The Behavioral Sciences: An Interpretation* (Reading, Mass.: Addison-Wesley, 1970).

With Ken McNeil, "The Regeneration of Social Organizations," *American Sociological Review*, vol. 36, August, 1971, pp. 624-637.

"Society's Frontiers for Organizing Activities," *Public Administration Review*, vol. 33, July/August, 1973, pp. 327-335.

With Walter Gove, James W. Grimm, and Susan Motz, "Family Economics and the Family Life Cycle: Internal Dynamics and Social Consequences," *Sociology and Social Research*, vol. 57, 1973, pp. 182-195.

"Technology, Polity, and Societal Development," *Administrative Science Quarterly*, vol. 19, March, 1974, pp. 6-21.

"Social Interdependence, the Polity and Public Administration," *Administration and Society*, vol. 6, May, 1974, pp. 3-21.

introduction to the transaction edition: thompson's bridge over troubled waters

You hold in your hands one of the half-dozen most influential books on organizations written in the twentieth century. James D. Thompson's *Organizations in Action* has significantly shaped the course of organization theory and research since its appearance in 1967. The value of this brilliant, elegant, concise treatise on organizations remains undiminished, and it is a pleasure to introduce it to a new generation of readers.

In this brief introduction, I undertake three tasks: (1) to portray the field of organizational studies before Thompson (BT); (2) to describe his seminal contributions (CT); and (3) to note developments in organization studies subsequent to his work (AT).

BT: ORGANIZATIONAL STUDIES BEFORE THOMPSON

Organizational studies has a long and checkered history, and did not emerge as a stable, recognized arena of scholarship until the mid-1950s. Work prior to that time consisted of four substantial contributions: the comparative studies of Max Weber, the scientific management work conducted by Frederick W. Taylor, the human relations studies associated with the work of Elton Mayo and William

Foote Whyte, and the adaptive system views of Chester Barnard and Philip Selznick.

Prior to 1950

The great social theorist Max Weber (1968 trans.), like many founding sociologists writing at the beginning of the twentieth century, endeavored to understand the changing bases of social order as a more traditional social structure rooted in shared culture, low mobility, and extended kinship ties gave way to a more mobile, differentiated, and impersonal order. Weber observed that the West was leading the way with the rise of the nation-state and its rapid industrialization overseen by corporate organizations. In Weber's formulation, rationalized legal and administrative systems were replacing traditional and charismatic modes of administration, and the rise of public- and private-sector bureaucracies were an important indicator and carrier of these new beliefs and values.

To a surprising extent, Frederick W. Taylor (1911) was observing and writing about the same great transformation. However, as an engineer of a more practical bent, Taylor focused primarily on changing approaches to production within factories, and rather than being content to describe and understand these developments, Taylor was deeply engaged in advancing them. In searching for "the one best way" to organize a task, Taylor began with the individual task and worker but quickly moved to consider ways to reform the entire production process, including front line supervisors and more distant managers. Taylor's ideas and approaches quickly spread to guide the reorganization of work in other arenas, such as schools and other service organizations. (Calahan 1962; Kanigel 1997) Both Weber and Taylor focused on efforts to rationalize production and administration.

By contrast, a collection of human relations scholars, reacting to what they saw as an overly individualist and rationalized conception of work and workers, conducted studies that led them to challenge the view that factories were simply production systems and workers economic entities. They noted the importance of social ties among workers (and later among managers), and documented the role of informal structure and non-rational motivations in organizing work. (See Mayo 1945; Whyte 1946) And, at a somewhat more macro level, Barnard (1938) and Selznick (1948) advanced the view of organizations as adaptive systems attempting to survive in their environment. Their functionalist approach emphasized that organizations are not simply technical systems, but political and social systems embodying norms and values of importance to their participants and to a wider circle of constituents.

It is only in retrospect that these strands of theory and research came to be viewed as forerunners of organization studies. Weber's work was long coded as

[handwritten margin note: Change in Weber's world]

"grand theory" or as that of an economic sociologist. Taylor was seen as a zealous engineer obsessed with time and motion studies and efficiency. And the human relations scholars were regarded as social scientists intent on demonstrating that generic social processes, such as informal control and commitment, operated within organizations just as they did in other social settings. Barnard and Selznick, by contrast, helped to point the way toward viewing organizations not simply as indicators of broader social trends or as settings for work, but as distinctive social systems—as collective actors—deserving of scholarly attention.

In a seminal essay from 1959, Alvin Gouldner surveyed the fledging field of organization studies and took an important step toward identifying major underlying fault-lines. Looking back on the efforts of Weber, Taylor, and the human relations analysts, Gouldner discerned two underlying models—a "rational" and a "natural" system perspective—that went far to account for much of the confusion and conflict among students of organizations. Rational system analysts regarded organizations as instruments that could be consciously shaped and molded to accomplish given ends. Emphasis was placed on rational design and planning under the assumption that participants can control developments. Natural system analysts, by contrast, viewed organizations as organic systems, as collectivities that evolve via spontaneous, indeterminant processes. System survival was seen as the overriding goal, and adaptation as the master process. Making explicit these underlying assumptions and contrasting models, somewhat paradoxically, allowed scholars to see more coherence in the field than had previously been visible. The recognition of a central debate with clearly defined protagonists spurred unity.

The identification of these competing conceptual models—rational and natural system perspectives—provided the first major blocks utilized by Thompson in crafting his own distinctive theoretical approach.

Enter Open Systems

Meantime, developments were occurring outside the social sciences that would act to reshape and redefine organization studies. During the mid 1950s, a broad intellectual movement termed "general systems theory" evolved under the leadership of biologists such as Ludwig von Bertalanffy, and information theorists such as W. Ross Ashby and Norbert Wiener. These scholars recognized that many scientific phenomena—from microorganisms to planets—operated as systems, but that these systems varied in level of complexity, reactivity, and degree of coupling. Kenneth Boulding (1956) was among the first to emphasize that organizations are open systems, characterized by a high level of complexity, reactivity, and looseness of coupling among system components. The open system conception directed the attention of scholars away from exclusive attention to internal features and processes toward recognizing the importance of organization-environmental connections. The most complete early application of open system arguments to organizations was provided by Katz and Kahn in their *The Social Psychology of Organizations* (1966).

The distinction between a closed system conception, which assumes that all elements and processes of interest are internal to the system being examined, and an open system perspective, which assumes that system structure and behavior are vitally, albeit variably, affected by environmental influences, provided the second set of building blocks for Thompson's conception. (For a more complete discussion of rational, natural and open system perspectives, see Scott 2003.)

CT: THOMPSON'S CONTRIBUTIONS

Decision Theory

The first work to recognize and begin to incorporate open-systems insights into organizational studies was the influential treatise by James G. March and Herbert Simon. Their book, simply entitled *Organizations,* commenced by boldly announcing:

Organizations are assemblages of interacting human beings and they are the largest assemblages in our society that have anything resembling a central coordinative system...the high specificity of structure and coordination within organizations—as contrasted with the diffuse and variable relations *among* organizations and among unorganized individuals—marks off the individual organization as a sociological unit comparable in significance to the individual organism in biology. (March and Simon 1958: 4)

Building upon the productive conceptual model initiated by Simon as early as 1945, March and Simon emphasized the extent to which organizational structures are crafted so as to simplify (for example, by subdividing) and support (for example, by providing specialized tools, training, and information) decision making by individuals within organizations. In *Organizations*, these models were extended and elaborated to take into account variations in the complexity and uncertainty posed by environment. For example, the amount of time and effort devoted by organizations to devising new rules and performance programs (i.e., innovation) vs. enacting existing ones, was explained by differences in rates of environmental change.

Two Contingency Models:

Variation among Organizations. This attention to effects of varying environments on microstructures was soon complemented by studies focused on more macrostructural features of organizations. One strand of this work argued that differing types of environments—varying levels of complexity and uncertainty—give rise to different types of organizations. Thus, an early study by Gouldner (1954) of a gypsum company contrasted the structuring of work and the patterning of rules in the two production spheres, mine and surface, as they reflected differences in the degree of danger and uncertainty confronted. Studies by Woodward (1958) of ninety-two industrial firms reported differences in their structural features depending on the complexity of technology employed. And Burns and Stalker (1961) examined twenty industrial firms, reporting that those with more turbulent and complex environments tended to develop that which they termed "organic" structures, while those in simpler and more stable environments adopted "mechanistic" structures characterized by higher levels of specialization and formalization.

This line of research culminated in the influential study by Lawrence and Lorsch (1967) of a half-dozen firms operating in three industries, each representing a different level of environmental complexity. Firms in more complex environments were more likely to be highly differentiated in structure and to devote more resources to coordination; firms in less complex environments were less differentiated and more easily integrated. In their concluding chapter, Lawrence and Lorsch reviewed previous theory and research, concluding that the ancient debate between rational and natural system theorists had been resolved. Both camps were right! Both were describing existing organizations. The differences in their perspectives reflected not differences in underlying assumptions or conceptual models employed, but differences in the types of organizations selected for study. Organizations are indeed open systems, and differences in their structures mirror differences in the environments to which they are attempting to adapt. They conclude:

This realization helps to explain the historical paradox posed earlier in this chapter—the parallel persistence of these two theories over a period of at least three decades. Both were needed to explain behavior in organizations operating in distinctly different environments; one theory could not displace the other. (p. 183)

Thompson contemplated the same paradox and arrived at a different resolution.
Variation within Organizations. Thompson proposed a "levels" model in which he suggests that (1) all organizations are, by their nature, open to the environment, (2) all organizations must adapt to their environments by crafting appro-

priate structures, but (3) organizations are differentiated systems, and some components or sub-units are designed to be more open—and some more closed—to environmental influences than others. Thompson embraced a three-level distinction developed by Parsons (1960), who differentiated among the production, managerial, and institutional components of organizations. Production components, if they are to be effective, should, to the extent possible, be sealed off from environmental changes. Numerous distinctive organizational sub-units and mechanisms develop to "buffer" the "technical core" from undue disturbances—to artificially close the system. On the other hand, organizations must attend and adapt to changes in their broader environments, and so a set of specialized units is created to monitor, incorporate, and attempt to influence critical suppliers of resources, markets, and sociopolitical agents. These units must be open to environmental signals. Managerial units must mediate between the more open organizational components that track environmental change and the more closed organizational units that attempt to carry on routinized production activities. In Thompson's imaginative model, all organizations are simultaneously rational and natural systems; and all are both open and closed systems.

In my view, both of these approaches to reconciliation have merit. On the one hand, it is clear that some organizations confront environmental influences that require them to be informal, flexible, and light-on-their-feet, celebrating the virtues of an open-natural system model, whereas other organizations confront more placid environments and can manage by simply performing routine activities in standardized ways of the sort proposed by rational system models. Thus, organizations vary in structural complexity and design in response to differences in their environments. On the other hand, it is also clear that organization structures are not all of a piece. They vary dramatically in the number, composition, and orientation of their sub-units. Some of these units are intended to be more open to environmental challenges, and others are designed to be protected from unexpected developments. Our understanding of the sources of structural variation of organizations is enhanced by both contingency perspectives.

However, Thompson's model has been especially productive in illuminating (1) the sources of differentiation and elaboration of organization structure; and (2) the types of mechanisms and strategies employed by organizations in adapting to their environments. In considering sources, Thompson points to the importance of the type of technology employed, the level of interdependence among the tasks performed, the degree of power/dependence characterizing the organization in relation to competitors and exchange partners, the stability and/or homogeneity of the environment, and the extent of ambiguity of standards employed to evaluate organizational performance. These varying conditions are linked to a number of organizational responses, including attempts to buffer components from environmental influences, attempts to construct bridges linking the organization to other players, types of coordination strategies, modes of assessment, and size of the dominant coalition. In combination, Thompson develops well over one hundred testable propositions linking environmental conditions to organizational features. His conceptual distinctions and propositions have provided a rich mother lode of ideas that subsequent organization scholars continue to mine.

AT: AFTER THOMPSON

In combination, the work of Lawrence and Lorsch and Thompson—their main contributions appearing in the same year (1967)—defined the contingency theory of organizations. It remains, arguably, the most influential theory of organizations to this day. The theory has been considerably elaborated in subsequent years. In particular, the Aston group (Pugh, Hickson, Hinings and Turner 1968) and Peter Blau and colleagues (e.g., Blau and Schoenherr 1971) examined the effects of size and environmental complexity on structure; Jay Galbraith (1973; 1977) developed arguments related to task complexity, information processing, and structural complexity; and Pfeffer and Salancik (1978) pursued the development of arguments relating to power/dependence relations among organizations. A subsequent generation of scholars has developed a "configurational" version that emphasizes that organizational adaptation is not driven by a single variable but by a combination of conditions giving rise to a complex structural response. (See Meyer, Tsui, and Hinings 1993) A recent treatise by Donaldson (2001) summarizes theoretical developments and empirical evidence.

A number of other theoretical perspectives have developed subsequent to Thompson's work, most notably, organization ecology and institutional theory. In many ways, these perspectives do not challenge contingency theory directly but rather redirect attention to "higher" levels of analysis, the organizational population (organizations utilizing the same form), and the organizational field (multiple types of organizations working in a common arena, e.g., mental health). However, the ecological approach questions the assumption of contingency theorists that organizations can readily change their structures to adapt to changing circumstances. They suggest that it is (more) often the case that new types of organizations arise to meet new circumstances rather than existing organizations altering their structures. (See Hannan and Freeman 1989) And institutional theorists point out that contin-

gency theorists privilege technical or task environments over institutional environments. They call attention to the ways in which legal systems, widely shared belief
systems, and norms define the environments of organizations and shape the response repertory available to any given organization. (See Scott, 2001)

Such developments can, perhaps, be incorporated into contingency theory.
But better, I think, to regard them as additional perspectives calling attention to
the diverse range of influences to which organizations are subject, and the multiple ways in which organizations relate to the wider social societal structures in
which they participate. The continuing relevance and influence of Thompson is
signaled by the recent effort of Kamps and Pólos (1999), who developed a formalized model of some of Thompson's key propositions. Their work is based on "the
feeling that Thompson's theory still has much to offer to contemporary scholars..." (p. 1805). I could not agree more.

w. richard scott
stanford university

REFERENCES

Barnard, Chester I. 1938. *The Functions of the Executive.* Cambridge, MA: Harvard
University Press.
Blau, Peter M. and Richard Schoenherr 1971. *The Structure of Organizations.*
New York: Basic Books.
Boulding, Kenneth E. 1956. "General Systems Theory: The Skeleton of Science,"
Management Science 2:197-208.
Burns, Tom and George M. Stalker 1961.*The Management of Innovation.* Lon-
don: Tavistock.
Calahan, R. E. 1962. *Education and the Cult of Efficiency: A Study of the Social
Forces that have Shaped the Administration of the Public Schools.* Chi-
cago: University of Chicago Press.
Donaldson, Lex 2001. *The Contingency Theory of Organizations.* Thousand Oaks,
CA: Sage Publications.
Galbraith, Jay R. 1973. *Designing Complex Organizations.* Reading, MA: Addison-
Wesley.
Galbraith, Jay R. 1977. *Organization Design.* Reading, MA: Addison-Wesley.

Gouldner, Alvin W. 1954. *Patterns of Industrial Bureaucracy.* Glencoe, IL: Free Press.

Hannan, Michael T. and John Freeman 1989. *Organizational Ecology.* Cambridge: Harvard University Press.

Kamps, Jaap and Lásló Pólos 1999. "Reducing Uncertainty: A Formal Theory of *Organizations in Action,*" *American Journal of Sociology* 104:1776-1812.

Kanagel, Robert 1997. *The One Best Way: Frederick Winslow Taylor and the Enigma of Efficiency.* New York: Viking.

Katz, Daniel and Robert L. Kahn 1966. *The Social Psychology of Organizations.* New York: Wiley.

Lawrence, Paul R. and Jay W. Lorsch 1967. *Organization and Environment: Managing Differentiation and Integration.* Boston: Graduate School of Business Administration, Harvard University.

March, James G. and Herbert A. Simon 1958. *Organizations.* New York: Wiley.

Mayo, Elton 1945. *The Social Problems of an Industrial Civilization.* Boston: Graduate School of Business Administration, Harvard University.

Meyer, Alan D., Anne S. Tsui, and C. R. Hinings 1993. "Configurational Approaches to Organizational Analysis," *Academy of Management Journal* 36:1175-1195.

Parsons, Talcott 1960. *Structure and Process in Modern Societies.* New York: Free Press of Glencoe.

Pfeffer, Jeffrey and Gerald R. Salancik 1978. *The External Control of Organizations.* New York: Harper & Row.

Pugh, D. S., D. J. Hickson, C. R. Hinings, and C. Turner 1968. "Dimensions of Organization Structure," *Administrative Science Quarterly* 14:91-114.

Scott, W. Richard 2001. *Institutions and Organizations,* 2nd ed. Thousand Oaks, CA: Sage Publications.

Scott, W. Richard 2003. *Organizations: Rational, Natural, and Open Systems,* 5th ed. Upper Saddle, NJ: Prentice-Hall.

Selznick, Philip 1948. "Foundations of the Theory of Organization," *American Sociological Review* 13:25-35.

Taylor, Frederick Winslow 1911. *The Principles of Scientific Management.* New York: Harper.

Weber, Max 1968 trans. *Economy and Society: An Interpretive Sociology,* 3 vols., Guenther Roth and Claus Wittich, eds. New York: Bedminister Pres (first published in 1924).

Whyte, William Foote, ed. 1946. *Industry and Society.* New York: McGraw-Hill.

Woodward, Joan 1958. *Management and Technology.* London: H.M.S.O.

preface

No useful theory can rest on the assumption that everything is unique. It is probably inevitable that the early history of a scientific endeavor will be characterized by the opposite assumption, and by the search for universals. This certainly has been the case with organization theory, which until recently has been preoccupied with discovering the essential elements of all complex organizations.

I believe it is a sign of relative maturity when a field begins to focus on patterned variations. The discovery of universal elements is necessary, but alone it provides a static understanding. To get leverage on a topic, we must begin to see some of the universal elements as capable of variation.

In these terms, I believe organization theory is beginning to mature, for a growing inventory of empirical studies makes possible comparisons and contrasts which reinforce the assumption of common elements, but more importantly suggests ways of conceiving of variables.

I have written this book to call attention to some of these developments, which tend to go unnoticed because we are encouraged to converse within disciplines, while organizations are multidisciplinary phenomena. A central purpose of this book is to identify a framework which might link at important points several of the now independent approaches to the understanding of complex organizations.

Because this is a broad if still shallow field, I have had to match task to talent by imposing some major constraints on myself:

1. Attention is limited to instrumental organizations which induce or coerce participation, and not to organizations of a "voluntary" nature, such as religious or ideological associations. Hopefully, some of the propositions advanced will apply to these as well, but I will not be explicit about them.

2. I have undertaken no obligation to portray faithfully the evolution of organization theories. Concepts are important, but for present purposes the sequence in which they appeared is not. Ideas are important; tracing them to their ultimate origins is another matter.

3. I have exercised considerable discretion, selecting those concepts which appear fruitful for present purposes and omitting all others, no matter how widely they are used or how powerful they have proved to be for other purposes. Only those which I could hook together have been used.

4. I have taken the liberty of extending or modifying some of the concepts found in existing literature. Whenever such liberties have been taken, I have tried to show the ways in which my usage differs from those cited.

Nice

This book might be considered a conceptual inventory. This is a departure from the recent fashion of conducting "propositional inventories," which assumes that important relationships have already been explored (Berelson and Steiner, 1964). I assume merely that the concepts relevant to important relationships exist, and once having identified some, I hope to generate potentially significant propositions. We lack the systematic evidence that eventually must come, but there are illustrative studies cited to indicate that the propositions are plausible. Most of my citations are of contemporary American organizations, but the intention has been to state propositions which are neither time- nor space-bound.

I assume that there are differences among organizations, and hope to account for some of them. But I also assume that there is not a one-to-one correspondence between significant organizational differences and the typical categories of business, government, medicine, and education. Likewise, I believe there is not a direct correlation between the academic disciplines and useful categories of complex organizations.

Illustrations are drawn from a variety of fields; and concepts from a variety of disciplines. I have carried concepts from one discipline into fields not typically studied with those concepts. I have tried to say more, using some concepts, than has typically been said with them. At the same time, I have said considerably less, using those same concepts, than has been said. The economist, sociologist, political scientist, or social psychologist will each find that I have overlooked refinements and intricacies of concepts he knows well. I have done so deliberately, in order to achieve a generality across typical categories of organizations. I hope, however, that I have avoided outright distortion of concepts.

My focus is on the behavior of organizations; behavior within organizations is considered only to the extent that it helps us understand organizations in the round. In order to focus attention on organizations as such, I have resorted in Part One to some verbal simplifications which are indefensible if taken literally. Specifically, in considering organizations as "actors," I employ terms usually associated with human actors—terms referring to purpose or motivation. I realize that organizations act only as the result of action by their members, and I deal explicitly with such matters in Part Two. Meanwhile, the reader is asked to consider such phrasings as shorthand conventions employed only temporarily to facilitate communication.

Of course, I hope that this book will be regarded as an original contribution, but the claim to originality is a difficult one to establish. In the building of a science, each of us starts with the contributions of others. Those familiar with organization theory in the mid-sixties will recognize that my debts fan out much further than specific citations indicate. But in addition to works in the public domain, I have profited personally and deeply from colaboration with colleagues Robert W. Avery, Frederick L. Bates, Richard O. Carlson, Peter B. Hammond, Robert W. Hawkes, William J. McEwen, and Arthur Tuden; and from my friends and teachers, N. J. Demerath and Edward H. Litchfield.

Organizations and administrators have been important to me. Had not the late Howard W. Odum built the department of sociology at the University of North Carolina, I could not have benefited from association with Fred Bates and Nick Demerath. Had not Litchfield had the vision to incorporate the social sciences into the Graduate School of Business and Public Administration at Cornell University, I would not have enjoyed association with Bill McEwen or continued learning from Fred Bates. And had not Litchfield established the Administrative Science Center at the University of Pittsburgh, I would not have been privileged to collaborate with Bob Avery, Dick Carlson, Peter Hammond, Bob

Hawkes, or Art Tuden; nor to learn by working with Carl Beck, Morris Ogul, and C. Edward Weber.

And were not Litchfield a master administrator, my understanding of organizations might never have extended beyond the boundaries of organizations; or my appreciation of administration beyond the mundane.

This entire manuscript was read carefully and critically by Arthur Stinchcombe and James Q. Wilson. Although I could not meet all of their criticisms, the book is immeasurably stronger for their comments.

james d. thompson

organizations in action

Organizations act, but what determines how and when they will act?

There is precedent for considering the organization as but the lengthened shadow of one or a few men. If this were adequate, our search for understanding could be focused narrowly on personality variables, which would simplify the task in the specific case but make generalization enormously difficult. Leaving room for the influence of the individual (which we will explore later), we will set aside the personality approach as deceptively simple and consider in Part One some of the impersonal forces which generate and guide the behavior of organizations.

We will argue that organizations do some of the basic things they do because they must—or else! Because they are expected to produce results, their actions are expected to be reasonable or rational. The concepts of rationality brought to bear on organizations establish limits within which organizational action must take place. We need to explore the meanings of these concepts and how they impinge on organizations.

Uncertainties pose major challenges to rationality, and we will argue that technologies and environments are basic sources of uncertainty for organizations. How these facts of organizational life lead organizations to design and structure themselves needs to be explored.

If this thesis rings true, then those organizations with similar technological and environmental problems should exhibit similar behavior;

patterns should appear. But if our thesis is fruitful, we should also find that patterned variations in problems posed by technologies and environments result in systematic differences in organizational action.

Our ability to find patterns in phenomena rests on the adequacy of the conceptual schemes we employ; that is, the kinds of answers we get are limited by the kinds of questions we ask. We begin our analysis of organizations in action with an inventory of the alternative conceptual schemes available to us.

strategies for studying organizations

Complex organizations—manufacturing firms, hospitals, schools, armies, community agencies—are ubiquitous in modern societies, but our understanding of them is limited and segmented.

The fact that impressive and sometimes frightening consequences flow from organizations suggests that some individuals have had considerable insight into these social instruments. But insight and private experiences may generate private understandings without producing a public body of knowledge adequate for the preparation of a next generation of administrators, for designing new styles of organizations for new purposes, for controlling organizations, or for appreciation of distinctive aspects of modern societies.

What we know or think we know about complex organizations is housed in a variety of fields or disciplines, and communication among them more nearly resembles a trickle than a torrent (Dill, 1964; March, 1965). Although each of the several schools has its unique terminology

3

and special heroes, Gouldner (1959) was able to discern two fundamental models underlying most of the literature. He labeled these the "rational" and "natural-system" models of organizations, and these labels are indeed descriptive of the results.

To Gouldner's important distinction we wish to add the notion that the rational model results from a *closed-system strategy* for studying organizations, and that the natural-system model flows from an *open-system strategy*.

CLOSED-SYSTEM STRATEGY

The Search for Certainty

If we wish to predict accurately the state a system will be in presently, it helps immensely to be dealing with a *determinate system*. As Ashby observes (1956), fixing the present circumstances of a determinate system will determine the state it moves to next, and since such a system cannot go to two states at once, the transformation will be unique.

Fixing the present circumstances requires, of course, that the variables and relationships involved be few enough for us to comprehend and that we have control over or can reliably predict all of the variables and relations. In other words, it requires that the system be closed or, if closure is not complete, that the outside forces acting on it be predictable.

Now if we have responsibility for the future states or performance of some system, we are likely to opt for a closed system. Bartlett's (1958) research on mental processes, comparing "adventurous thinking" with "thinking in closed systems," suggests that there are strong human tendencies to reduce various forms of knowledge to the closed-system variety, to rid them of all ultimate uncertainty. If such tendencies appear in puzzle-solving as well as in everyday situations, we would especially expect them to be emphasized when responsibility and high stakes are added.

Since much of the literature about organizations has been generated as a by-product of the search for improved efficiency or performance, it is not surprising that it employs closed-system assumptions—employs the rational model—about organizations. Whether we consider *scientific management* (Taylor, 1911), *administrative management* (Gulick and Urwick, 1937), or *bureaucracy* (Weber, 1947), the ingredients of the organization are deliberately chosen for their necessary contribution to a goal, and the structures established are those deliberately intended to attain highest efficiency.

Three Schools in Caricature

Scientific management, focused primarily on manufacturing or similar production activities, clearly employs economic efficiency as its ultimate criterion, and seeks to maximize efficiency by planning procedures according to a technical logic, setting standards, and exercising controls to ensure conformity with standards and thereby with the technical logic. Scientific management achieves conceptual closure of the organization by assuming that goals are known, tasks are repetitive, output of the production process somehow disappears, and resources in uniform qualities are available.

Administrative-management literature focuses on structural relationships among production, personnel, supply, and other service units of the organization; and again employs as the ultimate criterion economic efficiency. Here efficiency is maximized by specializing tasks and grouping them into departments, fixing responsibility according to such principles as span of control or delegation, and controlling action to plans. Administrative management achieves closure by assuming that ultimately a master plan is known, against which specialization, departmentalization, and control are determined. (That this master plan is elusive is shown by Simon, 1957.) Administrative management also assumes that production tasks are known, that output disappears, and that resources are automatically available to the organization.

Bureaucracy also follows the pattern noted above, focusing on staffing and structure as means of handling clients and disposing of cases. Again the ultimate criterion is efficiency, and this time it is maximized by defining offices according to jurisdiction and place in a hierarchy, appointing experts to offices, establishing rules for categories of activity, categorizing cases or clients, and then motivating proper performance of expert officials by providing salaries and patterns for career advancement. [The extended implications of the assumptions made by bureaucratic theory are brought out by Merton's (1957) discussion of "bureaucratic personality."] Bureaucratic theory also employs the closed system of logic. Weber saw three holes through which empirical reality might penetrate the logic, but in outlining his "pure type" he quickly plugged these holes. Policymakers, somewhere above the bureaucracy, could alter the goals, but the implications of this are set aside. Human components—the expert officeholders—might be more complicated than the model describes, but bureaucratic theory handles this by divorcing the individual's private life from his life as an officeholder through the use of rules, salary, and career. Finally, bureaucratic theory takes note of outsiders—clientele—but nullifies their effects by depersonalizing and categorizing clients.

It seems clear that the rational-model approach uses a closed-system strategy. It also seems clear that the developers of the several schools using the rational model have been primarily students of performance or efficiency, and only incidentally students of organizations. Having focused on control of the organization as a target, each employs a closed system of logic and conceptually closes the organization to coincide with that type of logic, for this elimination of uncertainty is the way to achieve determinateness. The rational model of an organization results in everything being functional—making a positive, indeed an optimum, contribution to the overall result. All resources are appropriate resources, and their allocation fits a master plan. All action is appropriate action, and its outcomes are predictable.

It is no accident that much of the literature on the management or administration of complex organizations centers on the concepts of *planning* or *controlling*. Nor is it any accident that such views are dismissed by those using the open-system strategy.

OPEN-SYSTEM STRATEGY

The Expectation of Uncertainty

If, instead of assuming closure, we assume that a system contains more variables than we can comprehend at one time, or that some of the variables are subject to influences we cannot control or predict, we must resort to a different sort of logic. We can, if we wish, assume that the system is determinate by nature, but that it is our incomplete understanding which forces us to expect surprise or the intrusion of uncertainty. In this case we can employ a natural-system model.

Approached as a natural system, the complex organization is a set of interdependent parts which together make up a whole because each contributes something and receives something from the whole, which in turn is interdependent with some larger environment. Survival of the system is taken to be the goal, and the parts and their relationships presumably are determined through evolutionary processes. Dysfunctions

Nominally

Not Darwinian!

are conceivable, but it is assumed that an offending part will adjust to produce a net positive contribution or be disengaged, or else the system will degenerate.

Central to the natural-system approach is the concept of homeostasis, or self-stabilization, which spontaneously, or naturally, governs the necessary relationships among parts and activities and thereby keeps the system viable in the face of disturbances stemming from the environment.

Two Examples in Caricature

Study of the *informal organization* constitutes one example of research in complex organizations using the natural-system approach. Here attention is focused on variables which are not included in any of the rational models—sentiments, cliques, social controls via informal norms, status and status striving, and so on. It is clear that students of informal organization regard these variables not as random deviations or error, but as patterned, adaptive responses of human beings in problematic situations (Roethlisberger and Dickson, 1939). In this view the informal organization is a spontaneous and functional development, indeed a necessity, in complex organizations, permitting the system to adapt and survive.

A second version of the natural-system approach is more global but less crystallized under a label. This school views the organization as a unit in interaction with its environment, and its view was perhaps most forcefully expressed by Chester Barnard (1938) and by the empirical studies of Selznick (1949) and Clark (1956). This stream of work leads to the conclusion that organizations are not autonomous entities; instead, the best laid plans of managers have unintended consequences and are conditioned or upset by other social units—other complex organizations or publics—on whom the organization is dependent.

Again it is clear that in contrast to the rational-model approach, this research area focuses on variables not subject to complete control by the organization and hence not contained within a closed system of logic. It is also clear that students regard interdependence of organization and enviroment as inevitable or natural, and as adaptive or functional.

CHOICE OR COMPROMISE?

The literature about organizations, or at least much of it, seems to fall into one of the two categories, each of which at best tends to ignore the other and at worse denies the relevance of the other. The logics associated with each appear to be incompatible, for one avoids uncertainty to achieve determinateness, while the other assumes uncertainty and indeterminateness. Yet the phenomena treated by each approach, as distinct from the explanations of each, cannot be denied.

Viewed in the large, complex organizations are often effective instruments for achievement, and that achievement flows from planned, controlled action. In every sphere—educational, medical, industrial, commercial, or governmental—the quality or costs of goods or services may be challenged and questions may be raised about the equity of distribution within the society of the fruits of complex organizations. Still millions live each day on the assumption that a reasonable degree of purposeful, effective action will be forthcoming from the many complex organizations on which they depend. Planned action, not random behavior, supports our daily lives. Specialized, controlled, patterned action surrounds us.

There can be no question but that the rational model of organizations directs our attention to important phenomena—to important "truth" in the sense that complex organizations viewed in the large exhibit some of the patterns and results to which the rational model attends, but which the natural-system model tends to ignore. But it is equally evident that phenomena associated with the natural-system approach also exist in complex organizations. There is little room to doubt the universal emergence of the informal organization. The daily news about labor-management negotiations, interagency jurisdictional squabbles, collusive agreements, favoritism, breeches of contract, and so on, are impressive evidence that complex organizations are influenced in significant ways by elements of their environments, a phenomenon addressed by the natural-system approach but avoided by the rational. Yet most versions of the natural-system approach treat organizational purposes and achievements as peripheral matters.

It appears that each approach leads to some truth, but neither alone affords an adequate understanding of complex organizations. Gouldner calls for a synthesis of the two models, but does not provide the synthetic model.

Meanwhile, a serious and sustained elaboration of Barnard's work (Simon, 1957a; March and Simon, 1958; Cyert and March, 1963) has produced a newer tradition which evades the closed- versus open-system dilemma.

A NEWER TRADITION

What emerges from the Simon-March-Cyert stream of study is the organization as a problem-facing and problem-solving phenomenon. The focus is on organizational processes related to choice of courses of action in an environment which does not fully disclose the alternatives available or the consequences of those alternatives. In this view, the organization has limited capacity to gather and process information or to predict consequences of alternatives. To deal with situations of such great complexity, the organization must develop processes for *searching* and *learning*, as well as for *deciding*. The complexity, if fully faced, would overwhelm the organization, hence it must set limits to its definitions of situations; it must make decisions in *bounded rationality* (Simon, 1957b). This requirement involves replacing the maximum-efficiency criterion with one of satisfactory accomplishment, decision making now involving *satisficing* rather than *maximizing* (Simon, 1957b).

These are highly significant notions, and it will become apparent that this book seeks to extend this "newer tradition." The assumptions it makes are consistent with the open-system strategy, for it holds that the processes going on within the organization are significantly affected by the complexity of the organization's environment. But this tradition also touches on matters important in the closed-system strategy: performance and deliberate decisions.

But despite what seem to be obvious advantages, the Simon-March-Cyert stream of work has not entirely replaced the more extreme strategies, and we need to ask why so many intelligent men and women in a position to make the same observations we have been making should continue to espouse patently incomplete views of complex organizations.

The Cutting Edge of Uncertainty

Part of the answer to that question undoubtedly lies in the fact that supporters of each extreme strategy have had different purposes in mind, with open-system strategists attempting to understand organizations per se, and closed-system strategists interested in organizations mainly as vehicles for rational achievements. Yet this answer does not seem completely satisfactory, for these students could not have been entirely unaware of the challenges to their assumptions and beliefs.

We can suggest now that rather than reflecting weakness in those who use them, the two strategies reflect something fundamental about the cultures surrounding complex organizations—the fact that our culture does not contain concepts for simultaneously thinking about rationality and indeterminateness. These appear to be incompatible concepts, and we have no ready way of thinking about something as half-closed, half-rational. One alternative, then, is the closed-system approach of ignoring uncertainty to see rationality; another is to ignore rational action in order to see spontaneous processes. The newer tradition with its focus on organizational coping with uncertainty is indeed a major advance. It is notable that a recent treatment by Crozier (1964) starts from the bureaucratic position but focuses on coping with uncertainty as its major topic.

Yet in directing our attention to processes for meeting uncertainty, Simon, March, and Cyert may lead us to overlook the useful knowledge amassed by the older approaches. If the phenomena of rational models are indeed observable, we may want to incorporate some elements of those models; and if natural-system phenomena occur, we should also benefit from the relevant theories. For purposes of this volume, then, *we will conceive of complex organizations as open systems, hence indeterminate and faced with uncertainty, but at the same time as subject to criteria of rationality and hence needing determinateness and certainty.*

THE LOCATION OF PROBLEMS

As a starting point, we will suggest that the phenomena associated with open- and closed-system strategies are not randomly distributed through complex organizations, but instead tend to be specialized by location. To introduce this notion we will start with Parsons' (1960) suggestion that organizations exhibit three distinct levels of responsibility and control—*technical, managerial,* and *institutional.*

In this view, every formal organization contains a suborganization whose "problems" are focused around effective performance of the technical function—the conduct of classes by teachers, the processing of income tax returns and the handling of recalcitrants by the bureau, the processing of material and supervision of these operations in the case of physical production. The primary exigencies to which the technical suborganization is oriented are those imposed by the nature of the technical task, such as the materials which must be processed and the kinds of cooperation of different people required to get the job done effectively.

The second level, the managerial, *services* the technical suborganization by (1) mediating between the technical suborganization and those who use its products—the customers, pupils, and so on—and (2) procuring the resources necessary for carrying out the technical functions. The managerial level *controls*, or administers, the technical suborganization (although Parsons notes that its control is not unilateral) by deciding such matters as the broad technical task which is to be performed, the scale of operations, employment and purchasing policy, and so on.

Finally, in the Parsons formulation, the organization which consists of both technical and managerial suborganizations is also part of a wider social system which is the source of the "meaning," legitimation, or higher-level support which makes the implementation of the organization's goals possible. In terms of "formal" controls, an organization may be relatively independent; but in terms of the meaning of the functions performed by the organization and hence of its "rights" to command resources and to subject its customers to discipline, it is never wholly independent. This overall articulation of the organization and the institutional structure and agencies of the community is the function of the third, or institutional, level of the organization.

Parsons' distinction of the three levels becomes more significant when he points out that at each of the two points of articulation between them there is a *qualitative* break in the simple continuity of "line" authority because the functions at each level are qualitatively different. Those at the second level are not simply lower-order spellings-out of the top-level functions. Moreover, the articulation of levels and of functions rests on a two-way interaction, with each side, by withholding its important contribution, in a position to interfere with the functioning of the other and of the larger organization.

If we now reintroduce the conception of the complex organization as an open system subject to criteria of rationality, we are in a position to speculate about some dynamic properties of organizations. As we suggested, the logical model for achieving complete technical rationality uses a closed system of logic—closed by the elimination of uncertainty. In practice, it would seem, the more variables involved, the greater the likelihood of uncertainty, and it would therefore be advantageous for an organization subject to criteria of rationality to remove as much uncertainty as possible from its *technical core* by reducing the number of variables operating on it. Hence if both resource-acquisition and output-disposal problems—which are in part controlled by environmental elements and hence to a degree uncertain or problematic—can be removed from the technical core, the logic can be brought closer to closure, and the rationality, increased.

Uncertainty would appear to be greatest, at least potentially, at the other extreme, the institutional level. Here the organization deals largely with elements of the environment over which it has no formal authority or control. Instead, it is subjected to generalized norms, ranging from formally codified law to informal standards of good practice, to public authority, or to elements expressing the public interest.

At this extreme the closed system of logic is clearly inappropriate. The organization is open to influence by the environment (and vice versa) which can change independently of the actions of the organization. Here an open system of logic, permitting the intrusion of variables penetrating the organization from outside, and facing up to uncertainty, seems indispensable.

If the closed-system aspects of organizations are seen most clearly at the technical level, and the open-system qualities appear most vividly at the institutional level, it would suggest that a significant function of the managerial level is to mediate between the two extremes and the emphases they exhibit. If the organization must approach certainty at the technical level to satisfy its rationality criteria, but must remain flexible and adaptive to satisfy environmental requirements, we might expect the managerial level to mediate between them, ironing out some irregularities stemming from external sources, but also pressing the technical core for modifications as conditions alter. One exploration of this notion was offered in Thompson (1964).

Possible Sources of Variation

Following Parsons' reasoning leads to the expectation that differences in technical functions, or *technologies*, cause significant differences among organizations, and since the three levels are interdependent, differences in technical functions should also make for differences at managerial and institutional levels of the organization. Similarly, differences in the institutional structures in which organizations are imbedded should make for significant variations among organizations at all three levels.

Relating this back to the Simon-March-Cyert focus on organizational processes of searching, learning, and deciding, we can also suggest that while these adaptive processes may be generic, the ways in which they proceed may well vary with differences in technologies or in environments.

RECAPITULATION

Most of our beliefs about complex organizations follow from one or the other of two distinct strategies. The closed-system strategy seeks certainty by incorporating only those variables positively associated with goal achievement and subjecting them to a monolithic control network. The open-system strategy shifts attention from goal achievement to survival, and incorporates uncertainty by recognizing organizational interdependence with environment. A newer tradition enables us to conceive of the organization as an open system, indeterminate and faced with uncertainty, but subject to criteria of rationality and hence needing certainty. With this conception the central problem for complex organizations is one of coping with uncertainty. As a point of departure, we suggest that organizations cope with uncertainty by creating certain parts specifically to deal with it, specializing other parts in operating under conditions of certainty or near certainty. In this case, articulation of these specialized parts becomes significant.

We also suggest that technologies and environments are major sources of uncertainty for organizations, and that differences in those dimensions will result in differences in organizations. To proceed, we now turn to a closer examination of the meaning of "rationality," in the context of complex organizations.

2

rationality in organizations

Instrumental action is rooted on the one hand in *desired outcomes* and on the other hand in *beliefs* about cause/effect relationships. Given a desire, the state of man's knowledge at any point in time dictates the kinds of variables required and the manner of their manipulation to bring that desire to fruition. To the extent that the activities thus dictated by man's beliefs are judged to produce the desired outcomes, we can speak of technology, or *technical rationality.*

Technical rationality can be evaluated by two criteria: instrumental and economic. The essence of the instrumental question is whether the specified actions do in fact produce the desired outcome, and the instrumentally perfect technology is one which inevitably achieves such results. The economic question in essence is whether the results are obtained with the least necessary expenditure of resources, and for this there is no absolute standard. Two different routes to the same desired outcome may be compared in terms of cost, or both may be compared with some abstract ideal, but in practical terms the evaluation of economy is relative to the state of man's knowledge at the time of evaluation.

We will give further consideration to the assessment of organizational

14

action in a later chapter, but it is necessary to distinguish at this point between the instrumental and economic questions because present literature about organizations gives considerable attention to the economic dimension of technology but hides the importance of the instrumental question, which in fact takes priority. The cost of doing something can be considered only after we know that the something can be done.

Complex organizations are built to operate technologies which are found to be impossible or impractical for individuals to operate. This does not mean, however, that technologies operated by complex organizations are instrumentally perfect. The instrumentally perfect technology would produce the desired outcome inevitably, and this perfection is approached in the case of continuous processing of chemicals or in mass manufacturing—for example, of automobiles. A less perfect technology will produce the desired outcome only part of the time; nevertheless, it may be incorporated into complex organizations, such as the mental hospital, because desire for the possible outcome is intense enough to settle for possible rather than highly probable success. Sometimes the intensity of desire for certain kinds of outcomes, such as world peace, leads to the creation of complex organizations such as the United Nations to operate patently imperfect technologies.

VARIATIONS IN TECHNOLOGIES

Clearly, technology is an important variable in understanding the actions of complex organizations. In modern societies the variety of desired outcomes for which specific technologies are available seems infinite. A complete but simple typology of technologies which has found order in this variety would be quite helpful. Typologies are available for industrial production (Woodward, 1965) and for mental therapy (Hawkes, 1962) but are not general enough to deal with the range of technologies found in complex organizations. Lacking such a typology, we will simply identify three varieties which are (1) widespread in modern society and (2) sufficiently different to illustrate the propositions we wish to develop.

The Long-linked Technology[1]

A long-linked technology involves serial interdependence in the sense that act Z can be performed only after successful completion of act Y,

---

[1] The notions in this section rest especially on conversations some years ago with Frederick L. Bates. For a different but somewhat parallel analysis of work flows, see Dubin, 1959.

which in turn rests on act X, and so on. The original symbol of technical rationality, the mass production assembly line, is of this long-linked nature. It approaches instrumental perfection when it produces a single kind of standard product, repetitively and at a constant rate. Production of only one kind of product means that a single technology is required, and this in turn permits the use of clear-cut criteria for the selection of machines and tools, construction of work-flow arrangements, acquisition of raw materials, and selection of human operators. Repetition of the productive process provides experience as a means of eliminating imperfections in the technology; experience can lead to the modification of machines and provide the basis for scheduled preventive maintenance. Repetition means that human motions can also be examined, and through training and practice, energy losses and errors minimized. It is in this setting that the scientific-management movement has perhaps made its greatest contribution.

The constant rate of production means that, once adjusted, the proportions of resources involved can be standardized to the point where each contributes to its capacity; none need be underemployed. This of course makes important contributions to the economic aspect of the technology.

The Mediating Technology

Various organizations have, as a primary function, the linking of clients or customers who are or wish to be interdependent. The commercial bank links depositors and borrowers. The insurance firm links those who would pool common risks. The telephone utility links those who would call and those who would be called. The post office provides a possible linkage of virtually every member of the modern society. The employment agency mediates the supply of labor and the demand for it.

Complexity in the mediating technology comes not from the necessity of having each activity geared to the requirements of the next but rather from the fact that the mediating technology requires operating in *standardized ways*, and *extensively*; e.g., with multiple clients or customers distributed in time and space.

The commercial bank must find and aggregate deposits from diverse depositors; but however diverse the depositors, the transaction must conform to standard terms and to uniform bookkeeping and accounting procedures. It must also find borrowers; but no matter how varied their needs or desires, loans must be made according to standardized criteria and on terms uniformly applied to the category appropriate to the particular borrower. Poor risks who receive favored treatment jeopardize bank solvency. Standardization permits the insurance organization to define categories of risk and hence to sort its customers or potential customers into appropriate aggregate categories; the insured who is not a qualified risk but is so defined upsets the probabilities on which insurance rests. The telephone company became viable only when the telephone became regarded as a necessity, and this did not occur until equipment was standardized to the point where it could be incorporated into one network. Standardization enables the employment agency to aggregate job applicants into categories which can be matched against standardized requests for employees.

Standardization makes possible the operation of the mediating technology over time and through space by assuring each segment of the organization that other segments are operating in compatible ways. It is in such situations that the bureaucratic techniques of categorization and impersonal application of rules have been most beneficial (Weber, 1947; Merton, 1957a).

The Intensive Technology

This third variety we label *intensive* to signify that a variety of techniques is drawn upon in order to achieve a change in some specific object; but the selection, combination, and order of application are determined by feedback from the object itself. When the object is human, this intensive technology is regarded as "therapeutic," but the same technical logic is found also in the construction industry (Stinchcombe, 1959) and in research where the objects of concern are nonhuman.

The intensive technology is most dramatically illustrated by the general hospital. At any moment an emergency admission may require some combination of dietary, x-ray, laboratory, and housekeeping or hotel services, together with the various medical specialties, pharmaceutical services, occupational therapies, social work services, and spiritual or religious services. Which of these, and when, can be determined only from evidence about the state of the patient.

In the construction industry, the nature of the crafts required and the order in which they can be applied depend on the nature of the object to be constructed and its setting; including, for example, terrain, climate, weather. Organized or team research may draw from a variety of scientific or technical skills, but the particular combination and the order of application depend on the nature of the problem defined.

The development of military combat teams, with a multiplicity of highly skilled capacities to be applied to the requirements of changing circumstances, represents a shift toward the intensive technology in military operations (Janowitz, 1959).

The intensive technology is a custom technology. Its successful employment rests in part on the availability of all the capacities potentially needed, but equally on the appropriate custom combination of selected capacities as required by the individual case or project.

Boundaries of Technical Rationality

Technical rationality, as a system of cause/effect relationships which lead to a desired result, is an abstraction. It is instrumentally perfect when it becomes a closed system of logic. The closed system of logic contains all relevant variables, and only relevant variables. All other influences, or *exogenous variables,* are excluded; and the variables contained in the system vary only to the extent that the experimenter, the manager, or the computer determines they should.

When a technology is put to use, however, there must be not only desired outcomes and knowledge of relevant cause/effect relationships, but also power to control the empirical resources which correspond to the variables in the logical system. A closed system of action corresponding to a closed system of logic would result in instrumental perfection in reality.

The mass production assembly operation and the continuous processing of chemicals are more nearly perfect, in application, than the other two varieties discussed above because they achieve a high degree of control over relevant variables and are relatively free from disturbing influences. Once started, most of the action involved in the long-linked technology is dictated by the internal logic of the technology itself. With the mediating technology, customers or clients intrude to make difficult the standardized activities required by the technology. And with the intensive technology, the specific case defines the component activities and their combination from the larger array of components contained in the abstract technology.

Since technical perfection seems more nearly approachable when the organization has control over all the elements involved,

Proposition 2.1:   Under norms of rationality, organizations seek to seal off their core technologies from environmental influences.

ORGANIZATIONAL RATIONALITY

When organizations seek to translate the abstractions called technologies into action, they immediately face problems for which the core technologies do not provide solutions.

Mass production manufacturing technologies are quite specific, *assuming* that certain inputs are provided and finished products are somehow removed from the premises before the productive process is clogged; but mass production technologies do not include variables which provide solutions to either the input- or output-disposal problems. The present technology of medicine may be rather specific if certain tests indicate an appendectomy is in order, if the condition of the patient meets certain criteria, and if certain medical staff, equipment, and medications are present. But medical technology contains no cause/effect statements about bringing sufferers to the attention of medical practitioners, or about the provision of the specified equipment, skills, and medications. The technology of education rests on abstract systems of belief about relationships among teachers, teaching materials, and pupils; but learning theories assume the presence of these variables and proceed from that point.

One or more technologies constitute the core of all purposive organizations. But this technical core is always an incomplete representation of what the organization must do to accomplish desired results. Technical rationality is a necessary component but never alone sufficient to provide *organizational rationality*, which involves acquiring the inputs which are taken for granted by the technology, and dispensing outputs which again are outside the scope of the core technology.

At a minimum, then, organizational rationality involves three major component activities: (1) input activities, (2) technological activities, and (3) output activities. Since these are interdependent, organizational rationality requires that they be appropriately geared to one another. The inputs acquired must be within the scope of the technology, and it must be within the capacity of the organization to dispose of the technological production.

Not only are these component activities interdependent, but both input and output activities are interdependent with environmental elements. Organizational rationality, therefore, never conforms to closed-system logic but demands the logic of an open system. Moreover, since the technological activities are embedded in and interdependent with activities which are open to the environment, the closed system can never be completely attained for the technological component. Yet we have offered the proposition that organizations subject to rationality norms seek to seal off their core technologies from environmental influences. How do we reconcile these two contentions?

Proposition 2.2: Under norms of rationality, organizations seek to buffer environmental influences by surrounding their technical cores with input and output components.

To maximize productivity of a manufacturing technology, the technical core must be able to operate as if the market will absorb the single kind of product at a continuous rate, and as if inputs flowed continuously, at a steady rate and with specified quality. Conceivably both sets of conditions could occur; realistically they do not. But organizations reveal a variety of devices for approximating these "as if" assumptions, with input and output components meeting fluctuating environments and converting them into steady conditions for the technological core.

Buffering on the input side is illustrated by the stockpiling of materials and supplies acquired in an irregular market, and their steady insertion into the production process. Preventive maintenance, whereby machines or equipment are repaired on a scheduled basis, thus minimizing surprise, is another example of buffering by the input component. The recruitment of dissimilar personnel and their conversion into reliable performers through training or indoctrination is another; it is most dramatically illustrated by basic training or boot camp in military organizations (Dornbusch, 1955).

Buffering on the output side of long-linked technologies usually takes the form of maintaining warehouse inventories and items in transit or in distributor inventories, which permits the technical core to produce at a constant rate, but distribution to fluctuate with market conditions.

Buffering on the input side is an appropriate and important device available to all types of organizations. Buffering on the output side is especially important for mass-manufacturing organizations, but is less feasible when the product is perishable or when the object is inextricably involved in the technological process, as in the therapeutic case.

Buffering of an unsteady environment obviously brings considerable advantages to the technical core, but it does so with costs to the organization. A classic problem in connection with buffering is how to maintain inventories, input or output, sufficient to meet all needs without incurring obsolescence as needs change. Operations research recently has made important contributions toward this problem of "run out versus obsolescence," both of which are costly.

Thus while a fully buffered technological core would enjoy the conditions for maximum technical rationality, organizational rationality may call for compromises between conditions for maximum technical efficiency and the energy required for buffering operations. In an unsteady environment, then, the organization under rationality norms must seek other devices for protecting its technical core.

Proposition 2.3: Under norms of rationality, organizations seek to smooth out input and output transactions.

[handwritten margin note: Adapt vs. influence external env.]

Whereas buffering absorbs environmental fluctuations, smoothing or leveling involves attempts to reduce fluctuations in the environment. Utility firms—electric, gas, water, or telephone—may offer inducements to those who use their services during "trough" periods, or charge premiums to those who contribute to "peaking." Retailing organizations faced with seasonal or other fluctuations in demand, may offer inducements in the form of special promotions or sales during slow periods. Transportation organizations such as airlines may offer special reduced fare rates on light days or during slow seasons.

Organizations pointed toward emergencies, such as fire departments, attempt to level the need for their services by activities designed to prevent emergencies, and by emphasis on early detection so that demand is not allowed to grow to the point that would overtax the capacity of the organization. Hospitals accomplish some smoothing through the scheduling of nonemergency admissions.

Although action by the organization may thus reduce fluctuations in demand, complete smoothing of demand is seldom possible. But a core technology interrupted by constant fluctuation and change must settle for a low degree of technical rationality. What other devices do organizations employ to protect core technologies?

Proposition 2.4: Under norms of rationality, organizations seek to anticipate and adapt to environmental changes which cannot be buffered or leveled.

If environmental fluctuations penetrate the organization and require the technical core to alter its activities, then environmental fluctuations are exogenous variables within the logic of technical rationality. To the extent that environmental fluctuations can be anticipated, however, they can be treated as *constraints* on the technical core within which a closed system of logic can be employed.

The manufacturing firm which can correctly forecast demand for a particular time period can thereby plan or schedule operations of its technical core at a steady rate during that period. Any changes in technical operations due to changes in the environment can be made at the end of the period on the basis of forecasts for the next period.

Organizations often learn that some environmental fluctuations are patterned, and in these cases forecasting and adjustment appear almost automatic. The post office knows, for example, that in large commercial centers large volumes of business mail are posted at the end of the business day, when secretaries leave offices. Recently the post office has attempted to buffer that load by promising rapid treatment of mail posted in special locations during morning hours. Its success in buffering is not known at this writing, but meanwhile the post office schedules its technical activities to meet known daily fluctuations. It can also anticipate heavy demand during November and December, thus allowing its input components lead time in acquiring additional resources.

Banks likewise learn that local conditions and customs result in peak loads at predictable times during the day and week, and can schedule their operations to meet these shifts (Argyris, 1954).

In cases such as these, organizations have amassed sufficient experience to know that fluctuations are patterned with a high degree of regularity or probability; but when environmental fluctuations are the result of combinations of more dynamic factors, anticipation may require something more than the simple projection of previous experience. It is in these situations that forecasting emerges as a specialized and elaborate activity, for which some of the emerging management-science or statistical-decision theories seem especially appropriate.

To the extent that environmental fluctuations are unanticipated they interfere with the orderly operation of the core technology and thereby reduce its performance. When such influences are anticipated and considered as constraints for a particular period of time, the technical core can operate as if it enjoyed a closed system.

Buffering, leveling, and adaptation to anticipated fluctuations are widely used devices for reducing the influence of the environment on the technological cores of organizations. Often they are effective, but there are occasions when these devices are not sufficient to ward off environmental penetration.

Proposition 2.5: When buffering, leveling, and forecasting do not protect their technical cores from environmental fluctuations, organizations under norms of rationality resort to rationing.

Rationing is most easily seen in organizations pointed toward emergencies, such as hospitals. Even in nonemergency situations hospitals may ration beds to physicians by establishing priority systems for nonemergency admissions. In emergencies, such as community disasters, hospitals may ration pharmaceutical dosages or nursing services by dilution—by assigning a fixed number of nurses to a larger patient population. Mental hospitals, especially state mental hospitals, may ration technical services by employing primarily organic-treatment procedures—electroshock, drugs, insulin—which can be employed more economically than psychoanalytic or *milieu* therapies (Belknap, 1956). Teachers and caseworkers in social welfare organizations may ration effort by accepting only a portion of those seeking service, or if not empowered to exercise such discretion, may concentrate their energies on the more challenging cases or on those which appear most likely to yield satisfactory outcomes (Blau, 1955).

But rationing is not a device reserved for therapeutic organizations. The post office may assign priority to first-class mail, attending to lesser classes only when the priority task is completed. Manufacturers of suddenly popular items may ration allotments to wholesalers or dealers, and if inputs are scarce, may assign priorities to alternative uses of those resources. Libraries may ration book loans, acquisitions, and search efforts (Meier, 1963).

Rationing is an unhappy solution, for its use signifies that the technology is not operating at its maximum. Yet some system of priorities for the allocation of capacity under adverse conditions is essential if a technology is to be instrumentally effective—if action is to be other than random.

The Logic of Organizational Rationality

Core technologies rest on closed systems of logic, but are invariably embedded in a larger organizational rationality which pins the technology to a time and place, and links it with the larger environment through input and output activities. Organizational rationality thus calls for an open-system logic, for when the organization is opened to environmental influences, some of the factors involved in organizational action become *constraints;* for some meaningful period of time they are not variables but fixed conditions to which the organization must adapt. Some of the factors become *contingencies,* which may or may not vary, but are not subject to arbitrary control by the organization.

Organizational rationality therefore is some result of (1) constraints which the organization must face, (2) contingencies which the organization must meet, and (3) variables which the organization can control.

RECAPITULATION

Perfection in technical rationality requires complete knowledge of cause/effect relations plus control over all of the relevant variables, or closure. Therefore, under norms of rationality (Prop. 2.1), organizations seek to seal off their core technologies from environmental influences. Since complete closure is impossible (Prop. 2.2), they seek to buffer environmental influences by surrounding their technical cores with input and output components.

Because buffering does not handle all variations in an unsteady environment, organizations seek to smooth input and output transactions (Prop. 2.3), and to anticipate and adapt to environmental changes which cannot be buffered or smoothed (Prop. 2.4), and finally, when buffering, leveling, and forecasting do not protect their technical cores from environmental fluctuations (Prop. 2.5), organizations resort to rationing.

These are maneuvering devices which provide the organization with some self-control despite interdependence with the environment. But if we are to gain understanding of such maneuvering, we must consider both the direction toward which maneuvering is designed and the nature of the environment in which maneuvering takes place. We will examine these questions in Chapter 3.

3

domains of organized action

In accounting for the produced automobile, we ultimately must take into consideration the mining of ore and the production of steel, the extraction and refining of petroleum, and the production of rubber or synthetic rubber, all of which are essential (within current technology) if an automobile is to roll from a factory. Along the way the firm may also receive contributions from others who make fabricating machinery and conveyor belts, or build factories, and still others who generate and distribute power and credit. Some automobile manufacturers include within their boundaries a larger proportion or different array of these essential activities than other such firms, but none is self-sufficient.

Consider the technology of treating medical ills. A fairly routine hospital case may now rely on a series of complex organizations which perform research, make pharmaceuticals, ship, store, and prepare medications. It involves use of the products of medical schools and nursing schools (which may be incorporated within the hospital), and of factories which construct x-ray apparatus or weave cloth to make sheets. Hospitals vary in the extent to which they include or exclude certain essential activities, but none is self-sufficient.

The overall technology of producing steel products involves the discovery and extraction of ore, its transportation to points where furnaces and power are concentrated, and the processing of ores into steel. Ultimately it includes the fabrication of steel into items for final consumption. An organization within the steel industry must establish some niche and some boundaries around that part of the total effort for which the organization takes initiative. For reasons to be discussed later, firms involved in extraction, ore transport, and the basic processing of steel seldom undertake the ultimate conversion of steel into products for final use. In any event, the steel firm is dependent on others along the way.

The essential point is that all organizations must establish what Levine and White (1961) have termed a "domain." In their study of relationships among health agencies in a community, domain consists of "claims which an organization stakes out for itself in terms of (1) diseases covered, (2) population served, and (3) services rendered." With appropriate modifications in the specifics of the definition—for example, substituting "range of products" for "diseases covered"—the concept of domain appears useful for the analysis of all types of complex organizations. Thus universities are universities, but their domains may range considerably; some offer astronomy courses, others do not; some serve local populations, others are international; some offer student housing and graduate education, others do not. No two firms in the oil industry are identical in terms of domain. Some refine petroleum, and market gasoline and other derivatives; others buy and market gasoline and oil. Some operate in a regional territory; others are national or international. Some provide credit cards; others are cash and carry. Prisons may be prisons at one level of analysis, but the concept of domain may prevent us from making inappropriate comparisons of prisons with very different domains.

Domain, Dependence, and Environment

In the final analysis the results of organizational action rest not on a single technology but upon a technological matrix. A complicated technology incorporates the products or results of still other technologies. Although a particular organization may operate several core technologies, its domain always falls short of the total matrix. Hence the organization's domain identifies the points at which the organization is dependent on inputs from the environment. The composition of that environment, the location within it of capacities, in turn determines upon whom the organization is dependent.

The organization may find that there is only one possible source for a particular kind of support needed, whereas for another there may be many alternatives; the capacity of the environment to provide the needed support may be dispersed or concentrated. Similarly, demand for that capacity may be concentrated or dispersed; there may or may not be competition for it. If the organization's need is unique or nearly so, we can say that demand for the input is concentrated; if many others have similar needs, we can say that the demand is dispersed.

Similar distinctions can be made on the output side of the organization. Its environment may contain one or many potential customers or clients, and the organization may be alone in serving them or it may be one of many competitors approaching the client or clients.

The extent to which the sources of input and output support coincide may also be important to the organization. The general hospital in a major metropolitan area may draw its financial support from one sector of the environment, its personnel inputs from another, and its clientele from still a different one; and there may be no interaction among these elements except via the hospital. The general hospital in a small community, however, may find that the necessary parties are functionally interdependent and interact regularly with respect to religious, economic, recreational, and governmental matters.

The public school usually finds its clientele and financial supporters concentrated, and the two interconnected. The municipal university may be in a similar situation, whereas the private university may collect financial inputs, students, faculty, and research data from quite varied and separated sources.

Task Environments

But the notion of environment turns out to be a residual one; it refers to "everything else." To simplify our analysis, we can adopt the concept of *task environment* used by Dill (1958) to denote those parts of the environment which are "relevant or potentially relevant to goal setting and goal attainment." Dill found the task environments of two Norwegian firms to be composed of four major sectors: (1) customers (both distributors and users); (2) suppliers of materials, labor, capital, equipment, and work space; (3) competitors for both markets and resources; and (4) regulatory groups, including governmental agencies, unions, and interfirm associations. With appropriate modifications of the specific referrents—for example, substituting "clients" for "customers" in some cases—we have a useful concept to work with, and one much more delimited in scope than environment. We are now working with those organizations in the environment which make a difference to the organization in question; Evan (1966) employs the term "organization set" for this purpose.

[The remaining environment can be set aside for a while, but we cannot discard it for two reasons: (1) patterns of culture can and do influence organizations in important ways, and (2) the environment beyond the task environment may constitute a field into which an organization may enter at some point in the future. We will consider both of these aspects later.]

Just as no two domains are identical, no two task environments are identical. Which individuals, which other organizations, which aggregates constitute the task environment for a particular organization is determined by the requirements of the technology, the boundaries of the domain, and the composition of the larger environment.

Task Environments and Domain Consensus

The establishment of domain cannot be an arbitrary, unilateral action. Only if the organization's claims to domain are recognized by those who can provide the necessary support, by the task environment, can a domain be operational. The relationship between an organization and its task environment is essentially one of exchange, and unless the organization is judged by those in contact with it as offering something desirable, it will not receive the inputs necessary for survival. The elements typically exchanged by the health organizations studied by Levine and White fall into three main categories: (1) referral of cases, clients, or patients; (2) giving or receiving of labor services encompassing the use of volunteers, lent personnel, and offering of instruction to personnel of other organizations; and (3) sending or receiving of resources other than labor services, including funds, equipment, case and technical information. The specific categories of exchange vary from one type of organization to another, but in each case, as they note, exchange agreements rest upon *prior consensus regarding domain.*

The concept of domain consensus has some special advantages for our analysis of organizations in action, for it enables us to deal with operational goals (Perrow, 1961a) without imputing to the organization the human quality of motivation and without assuming a "group mind," two grounds on which the notion of organizational goals has been challenged.

Domain consensus defines a set of expectations both for members of an organization and for others with whom they interact, about what the organization will and will not do. It provides, although imperfectly, an image of the organization's role in a larger system, which in turn serves as a guide for the ordering of action in certain directions and not in others. Using the concept of domain consensus, we need not assume that the formal statement of goals found in charters, articles of incorporation, or institutional advertising is in fact the criterion upon which rationality is judged and choices of action alternatives are made. Nor need we accept such ideologies as that which insists that profit is the goal of the firm. The concept of domain consensus can be clearly separated from individual goals or motives. Regardless of these, members of hospitals somehow conceive of their organizations as oriented around medical care, and this conception is reinforced by those with whom the members interact. Members of regulatory agencies likewise conceive of a jurisdiction for their organizations, and members of automobile manufacturing firms conceive of production and distribution of certain kinds of vehicles as the organization's excuse for existence.

MANAGEMENT OF INTERDEPENDENCE

Task environments of complex organizations turn out to be multifaceted or pluralistic, composed of several or many distinguishable others potentially relevant in establishing domain consensus. This appears to be true even of organizations embedded in totalitarian politico-economic systems, since for any specific organization there appears to be alternative sources of some inputs; the several kinds of inputs required come under the jurisdictions of different state agencies; and there are alternative forms of output or places for disposal of output (Berliner, 1957; Granick, 1959; Richman, 1963). The evidence is inescapable that elaborate state planning and decrees do not fully settle for specific industrial organizations in the Soviet Union the questions of domain and domain consensus.

This pluralism of task environments is significant for complex organizations because it means that an organization must exchange with not one but several elements, each of which is itself involved in a network of interdependence, with its own domain and task environment. In the process of working out solutions to its problems, an element of the task environment may find it necessary or desirable to discontinue support to an organization. Thus task environments pose contingencies for organizations.

Task environments also impose constraints. The capacities of supporting organizations and the absence of feasible alternatives may fix absolute limits to the support which may be available to an organization at a given time. The most dramatic example of constraints, perhaps, arises in the case of governmental organizations which are captives of a particular population. The public school system treated badly by its mandatory population may lose some of its members, but the organization as such cannot move to another community; it must stay home and fight the "in-law" battle. The foreign office of a world power cannot elect to negotiate in another, rosier world. The captive organization exists in the business world, as well, in the form of the satellite or subsidiary firm, or the firm which produces for a single buyer, as in the missile business during the 1950s. Carlson (1961) notes that some organizations have no control over selection of clientele, and that the clientele likewise lacks an option. He refers to these as "domesticated" because they are not compelled to attend to all of their needs, society guaranteeing their existence.

Since the dependence of an organization on its task environment introduces not only constraints but also contingencies, both of which interfere with the attainment of rationality, we would expect organizations subject to norms of rationality to attempt to manage dependency.

Power and Dependence

Building on a conception advanced by Richard Emerson (1962), we can say that an organization is dependent on some element of its task environment (1) in proportion to the organization's need for resources or performances which that element can provide and (2) in inverse proportion to the ability of other elements to provide the same resource or performance. Thus a manufacturing firm is dependent on a financial organization to the extent that the firm needs financial resources, and financial resources are not available from other sources. The hospital is dependent on physicians in the community to the extent that the hospital needs patients and that physicians monopolize the capacity to refer patients to hospitals.

Emerson points out that dependence can be seen as the obverse of power. Thus an organization has power, relative to an element of its task environment, to the extent that the organization has capacity to satisfy needs of that element and to the extent that the organization monopolizes that capacity.

This approach to dependence and power has several advantages for our analysis of complex organizations and their domains. It frees us from the necessity of viewing power as some generalized attribute of the organization, and leads us to consider net power as resulting from a set of relationships between the organization and the several elements of its pluralistic task environment. Thus an organization may be relatively powerful in relation to those who supply its inputs and relatively powerless in relation to those who receive its outputs, or vice versa. Or an organization may be relatively powerful in relation to both input and output sectors, a situation which may generate "countervailing power" (Galbraith, 1958) in the form, for example, of new or strengthened regulatory agencies which become part of its task environment (Palamountain, 1955).

An organization may be relatively powerless on all sectors of its task environment, as Burton Clark (1956) has shown in his study of an adult education organization. This organization rested on "precarious values," in the sense that none of the important elements of its environment was fully committed to adult education as a high-priority activity. The organization therefore had to cater to whatever fleeting interests of an unstable population it could activate at a particular time, had to scrounge for resources, and could not develop a sustained domain consensus which would have facilitated planning for efficiency.

An organization may have power with respect to competitors if it has ability to act without regard for their actions; i.e., if competitors do not pose contingency factors for the organization. In the business sphere this is illustrated by the phenomenon of "price leadership," where it appears that no matter what action the price leader takes, it will be copied by followers. This situation also illustrates that an organization may be powerful in its task environment whether this is advantageous or not; for instance, being the price leader may be embarrassing in an environment which suspects collusion in such situations, and which contains regulatory agencies to penalize collusion. One of the advantages of the definition of power we have chosen is that it does not rest on any assumptions of intent or usage.

Finally, the power-dependence concept advanced here provides an important escape from the "zero-sum" concept of power (Emerson, 1962; Parsons, 1960), which assumes that in a system composed of A and B, the power of A is power at the expense of B. By considering power in the context of interdependence, we admit the possibility of A and B becoming increasingly powerful with regard to each other—the possibility that increasing interdependence may result in increased net power. It is this possibility on which coalitions rest.

The hospital, for example, may be quite dependent on referring physicians who control the supply of patients, and we would say that physicians are powerful with respect to the hospital. At the same time, if the hospital is the only one available or is sufficiently superior to others, physicians may be highly dependent on the hospital, and we would say that the hospital was powerful with respect to physicians. Thus the conception of power as rooted in dependence permits us to consider power in non-zero-sum terms.

The Competitive Strategy

We noted earlier that the task environment is defined by the dependence of the organization. Since dependence introduces constraints or contingencies, the problem for the organization is to avoid becoming subservient to elements of the task environment.

Proposition 3.1: Under norms of rationality, organizations seek to minimize the power of task-environment elements over them by maintaining alternatives.

To the extent that the needed capacity is dispersed through the task environment, the organization may develop alternative sources. By scattering its dependence, it prevents the concentration of power over it. It need not concede power to a single element of the task environment. (This maneuver sometimes encourages the several suppliers to coalesce into a united front, thus gaining power through its concentration. Cartels are an example.) We might expect, for example, that under favorable conditions the organization would practice exchanging with each of its several possible sources, thus establishing with each a precedent for support if conditions become less favorable (Kriesberg, 1955).

Now if the task environment contains not only many elements with the needed capacity but also many elements requiring such capacity, we are at or near the point which economists describe as perfect competition, when sufficient numbers of suppliers and demanders make the actions of any one insignificant. We would expect organizations to elect to compete under such conditions, for the organization knows that support will be available when needed and that it can maintain its freedom from commitment by negotiating an exchange each and every time a need occurs.

In reality, however, conditions of perfect competition are infrequent and highly unstable over time; and even if the organization faces perfect competition in one sector—for example, in disposing of its output—it may face imperfect competition in other sectors—for example, the recruitment of personnel. Competition in an imperfect market introduces considerable contingency, for it forces the relevant elements of the task environment to seek alternative sources of exchange, and thereby raises the possibility of losing out on any particular negotiation to such "third parties." Each time the organization needs a particular kind of support, it offers something in exchange; but if the elements of the task environment which control that support have better offers, the organization may be without a source of supply. Buffering capacity may reduce the severity of this problem (Prop. 2.2), but does not eliminate it.

If the organization engaged in competing for its needs must assume imperfect competition, in which the actions of (large) elements in the market can make significant differences, it becomes advisable to skew the imbalance in the organization's favor.

Proposition 3.2: Organizations subject to rationality norms and competing for support seek prestige.

Acquiring prestige is the "cheapest" way of acquiring power. To the extent that an environmental element finds it prestigeful to exchange with an organization, the organization has gained a measure of power over that element without making any commitments; i.e., it has gained power without yielding power. The importance of prestige is underscored in the study of a voluntary general hospital by Perrow (1961), who sees the creation and maintenance of a "favorable image of the organization in its salient publics" as an important way of controlling dependency. Perrow concludes that if an organization and its products are well regarded, it may more easily attract personnel, influence relevant legislation, wield informal power in the community, and ensure adequate numbers of clients, customers, donors, or investors. Litwak and Hylton (1962) found that welfare organizations which could establish distinctive bases for raising funds could reduce their dependency on other agencies in the community and thereby resist efforts to incorporate them into Community Chest programs.

The fostering of prestigeful images is widely evident among business firms, universities, and government agencies.

Proposition 3.3: When support capacity is concentrated in one or a few elements of the task environment, organizations under norms of rationality seek power relative to those on whom they are dependent.

We are not asserting that organizations with power will necessarily exercise or flaunt it, nor that the desire for power provides personal motives for individuals holding responsibilities at the institutional level of the organization. The proposition does assume, however, that power is a way of handling what would otherwise be serious contingencies, and that rationality is not achieved by completely powerless (dependent) organizations. We would expect, therefore, that organizations subject to rationality norms and constrained by monopolized or nearly monopolized capacity for support, will maneuver toward achieving power to offset their dependence. The question is how to achieve such power.

THE ACQUISITION OF POWER

Complex organizations "acquire" dependence when they establish domains, but the acquisition of power is not so easy. Organizations may, however, trade on the fact that other organizations in their task environments also have problems of domain and face constraints and contingencies. In the management of this interdependence, organizations employ cooperative strategies (Thompson and McEwen, 1958). As Cyert and March (1963) conclude, organizations avoid having to anticipate environmental action (Prop. 2.4) by arranging negotiated environments.

Cooperative Strategies

Using cooperation to gain power with respect to some element of the task environment, the organization must demonstrate its *capacity to reduce uncertainty* for that element, and *must make a commitment* to exchange that capacity.

Thus an agreement between A and B, specifying that A will supply and B will purchase, reduces uncertainty for both. A knows more about its output targets, and B knows more about its inputs. Likewise, the affiliation of a medical practitioner with a hospital reduces uncertainty for both. The medical practitioner has increased assurance that his patients will have bed and related facilities, and the hospital has increased assurance that its facilities will be used.

Convincing an environmental element of the organization's capacity to satisfy future needs is enhanced by historical evidence; prior satisfactory performance tends to suggest satisfactory performance in the future, and we might expect the organization to prefer to maintain an on-going relationship rather than establish a new one for the same purpose.

Under cooperative strategies, the effective achievement of power rests on the exchange of commitments, the reduction of potential uncertainty for both parties. But commitments are obtained by giving commitments and uncertainty, reduced for the organization through its reduction of uncertainty for others. Commitment thus is a double-edged sword, and management of interdependence presents organizations with dilemmas. Contracting, coopting, and coalescing represent different degrees of cooperation and commitment, and present organizations with alternatives.

Contracting refers here to the negotiation of an agreement for the exchange of performances in the future. Our usage is not restricted to those agreements which legal bodies would recognize. It includes agreements formally achieved between labor and industrial management via collective bargaining, but it also includes the understanding between a police department and minor criminals to forego prosecution in exchange for information about more important criminal activities. It also covers the understanding between a university and a donor involving, for example, the naming of buildings or the awarding of honorary degrees. Contractual agreements thus may rest on faith and the belief that the other will perform in order to maintain a reputation or prestige (Prop. 3.2), or they may depend on institutional patterns whereby third parties can be depended upon to evaluate fulfillment of obligations and assess penalties for failure (Macaulay, 1963).

Coopting has been defined (Selznick, 1949) as the process of absorbing new elements into the leadership or policy-determining structure of an organization as a means of averting threats to its stability or existence. Cooptation increases the certainty of future support by the organization coopted. The acceptance on the corporation's board of directors of representatives of financial institutions, for example, increases the likelihood of access to financial resources for the duration of the cooptive arrangement. But coopting is a more constraining form of cooperation than contracting, for to the extent that cooptation is effective it places an element of the environment in a position to raise questions and perhaps exert influence on other aspects of the organization.

Coalescing refers to a combination or joint venture with another organization or organizations in the environment. A coalition may be unstable, or may have a stated terminal point; but to the extent that it is operative, the organizations involved act as one with respect to certain operational goals. Coalition not only provides a basis for exchange but also requires a commitment to future joint decision making. It is therefore a more constraining form of cooperation than coopting.

Proposition 3.3 said that when support capacity is concentrated within few elements in the task environment, organizations under norms of rationality seek power relative to those on whom they are dependent. We can refine that proposition somewhat, using the distinctions just introduced relative to degrees of cooperation and commitment.

Proposition 3.3a: When support capacity is concentrated *and balanced against concentrated demands* the organizations involved will attempt to handle their dependence through contracting.

Proposition 3.3b: When support capacity is concentrated *but demand dispersed,* the weaker organization will attempt to handle its dependence through coopting.

Proposition 3.3c: When support capacity is concentrated and balanced against concentrated demands, but the power achieved through contracting is inadequate, the organizations involved will attempt to coalesce.

DEFENSE OF DOMAIN

The attainment of a viable domain is, in essence, a political problem. It requires finding and holding a position which can be recognized by all of the necessary "sovereign" organizations as more worthwhile than available alternatives. It requires establishing a position in which diverse organizations in diverse situations find overlapping interests. The management of interorganizational relations is just as political as the management of a political party or of international relationships. It can also be just as dynamic, as environments change and propel some elements out of and new elements into a task environment.

And just as political parties and world powers move toward their objectives through compromise, complex purposive organizations find compromise inevitable. The problem is to find the optimum point between the realities of interdependence with the environment and the norms of rationality.

Proposition 3.4:   The more sectors in which the organization subject to rationality norms is constrained, the more power the organization will seek over remaining sectors of its task environment.

The public school, for example, which is constrained to accept virtually all students of a specified age, under conditions of population growth has urgent need for power with respect to those in the task environment who control financial and other inputs. If the task environment imposes mandatory loads, the school must seek power with respect to resources. The private school, on the other hand, may be able to treat both student load and inputs as variables, and seek their mutual adjustment.

The business firm constrained by an impoverished market, as during a recession, finds it urgent to have power to curtail the rate and price of inputs provided by supply elements of the task environment. To the extent that it has power, it may renegotiate contractual arrangements. If the firm is also constrained by large fixed costs, as in heavy industries, our proposition would predict that the organization will seek power to curtail the flow of labor inputs. It is in such industries that wage payments typically are in hourly or piece rates, and firms are not committed to fixed salaries or guaranteed annual wages. By contrast, in the university, where variations in student load occur primarily at only one time of the year, wage payments are in annual terms.

Proposition 3.5: The organization facing many constraints and unable to achieve power in other sectors of its task environment will seek to enlarge the task environment.

Captive organizations frequently find themselves boxed in on several sides, to the point where norms of rationality are threatened or overwhelmed. It is at this point that captive organizations often join forces to establish noncaptive, evaluating organizations which develop yardsticks of rationality and set standards for accreditation. Community hospitals, prisons, city governments, and public schools all exhibit this device of creating new elements in the task environment to offset other constraints within it. To the extent that the new element has power to confer or withhold prestige, it can loosen the constraints operating on the organization (Prop. 3.2). The nonaccredited school or hospital, for example, may be threatened with irreplaceable loss of personnel, to the point where those who control financial inputs are forced to increase their support.

RECAPITULATION

The domain claimed by an organization and recognized by its environment determines the points at which the organization is dependent, facing both constraints and contingencies. To attain any significant measure of self-control, the organization must manage its dependency. Under norms of rationality, therefore (Prop. 3.1), organizations seek to minimize the power of task-environment elements over them by maintaining alternatives. When competing for support (Prop. 3.2), organizations seek prestige, which is a way of gaining power without increasing dependency.

Often, however, the environment does not offer many alternative sources of support. When support capacity is concentrated in the task environment (Prop. 3.3), organizations seek power relative to those on whom they are dependent. Subject to the nature of the interdependence, the organizations may resort to contracting, coopting, or coalescing.

The more an organization is constrained in some sectors of its task environment (Prop. 3.4), the more power it will seek over remaining elements of its task environment. When the organization is unable to achieve such a balance (Prop. 3.5), it will seek to enlarge its task environment.

From the point of view of a rational model of organizations, the compromises and maneuvering in defense of domains are disruptive and costly. We would therefore expect organizations subject to norms of rationality to seek to design themselves so as to minimize the necessity of maneuvering and compromise. We will consider the design of organizations in the next chapter.

4

organizational design

Organizational rationality is rooted in both technology and task environment. Given a domain, these variables define major constraints and contingencies for an organization. We have indicated several strategies available to organizations for meeting important contingencies, and have suggested that they entail varying degrees of commitment and curtailed freedom. Now we can suggest that in addition to dealing with contingencies through strategies for interaction, organizations may remove or reduce contingencies through organizational design.

Proposition 4.1: Organizations under norms of rationality seek to place their boundaries around those activities which if left to the task environment would be crucial contingencies.

The implication of this proposition is that we should expect to find organizations including within their domains activities or competencies which, on a technological basis, could be performed by the task environment without damage to the *major mission* of the organization. For the hotel, for example, provision of rooms and meals would be the major mission, and the operation of a laundry would be excluded; yet we find hotels operating laundries. On the other hand, provision of rooms and meals would not be within the major mission of the hospital, although hospitals commonly include these activities within their domains.

The incorporation of subsidiary competencies along with major missions is commonplace in organizations of all types and is not a major discovery. But our proposition is not an announcement of the fact; rather it attempts to indicate the direction in which domains are expanding. Since we are arguing that such expansion will be in the direction of crucial contingencies, and that crucial contingencies are located by the technology and the task environment, we can be somewhat more precise in suggesting the direction of expansion of organizations, depending on the type of technology required by the major mission.

In examining the concept of organizational domain, we have noted that domain is defined by (1) technology included, (2) population served, and (3) services rendered. Major changes in design involve modifications of the "mix" of these three elements.

Proposition 4.1a: Organizations employing long-linked technologies and subject to rationality norms seek to expand their domains through *vertical integration.*

The concept of vertical integration is significant in economics but seldom employed in other disciplines, perhaps because it applies primarily to long-linked technologies, and these appear most prominently in industrial areas. It refers to the combination in one organization of successive stages of production; each stage of production uses as its inputs the product of the preceding stage and produces inputs for the following stage. Technologically, each stage could be incorporated in a separate organization, and in fact much though not all vertical integration in industry occurs through the amalgamation into one organization of formerly discrete organizations. The literature of economic history is rich in examples of vertical integration.

The major American oil firms, for example, were refining organizations, but eventually integrated *forward* by establishing competence in marketing—i.e., handling their own output problems—and integrated *backward* by acquiring control over supplies of crude oil and marine transportation services—i.e., handling their own input problems. As automobile manufacturers developed mass production they also established marketing channels for mass distribution, and acquired capacity to make parts and accessories in order to have assured stocks of supplies when needed and at reasonable prices. Soon after accomplishing the technology for commercial production of aluminum, Alcoa moved into the making and marketing of finished products in order to develop demand for the product, and obtained bauxite mines, ore ships, and warehouses. [For a major treatment of this aspect of economic history, see Chandler (1927), from whom these examples are taken.]

Vertical integration, however, is not simply an historical phenomenon; it is a current movement of many industrial organizations in a variety of fields. With the recent shrinkage of profit margins, which led to renewed emphasis on rationality norms, major meat packers have moved backward behind the livestock auction markets to establish contractual relationships with livestock feeders. By owning the livestock and feed, and contracting to have livestock fed, the packers can control the flow of animals into slaughterhouses and can calculate their costs in advance, both of which are serious contingencies when packers depend on irregular volume and fluctuating prices in auction markets.

Vertical integration thus is a major way of expanding organizational domains in order to reduce or eliminate significant contingencies. It is most feasible when the underlying technology is long linked, with each activity dependent on the one preceding it and providing a needed input to the one following. Thus it is most feasible in manufacturing industries, rather than in those employing mediating or intensive technologies. Still, hospitals became not only organizations providing health care, but also educational organizations to assure the future provision of highly trained personnel; hospitals often operate nursing schools and internship programs.

Even when a sequential relationship in the several stages of production does exist, there may be other limits to vertical integration which prevent organizations from becoming self-sufficient. Perhaps the most important limitation occurs when the activities which precede or follow a major mission *fan out* rapidly. Basic steel producers may integrate forward to fabricate that product into some of its structural forms, but find it impossible to engage in the manufacture and distribution of all the ultimate products—such as automobiles—which contain steel. Organizations whose primary missions fall at the other end of the scheme, in distribution, frequently find backward integration difficult because of rapid fanning out. Sears, Roebuck, for example, would find it inconceivable to engage in the many technologies required for the manufacture of the variety Sears offers its customers. The inputs for Sears fan out too quickly. It is reported, however, that Sears did occasionally (and reluctantly) help finance manufacturing companies or purchase portions of their stock in order to assure itself of adequate supplies (Chandler, 1962); and it has moved backward to incorporate warehousing and transportation components.

Whenever the activities behind or ahead of an organization fan out rapidly, we would expect vertical integration to be highly selective, concentrating on those support activities which appear to be strategic or crucial.

Proposition 4.1b: Organizations employing mediating technologies, and subject to rationality norms seek to expand their domains by increasing the populations served.

Such expansion may be territorial or saturative, or both. The historical movement is well documented in the case of transport organizations and public utilities. Railroad and airline firms rushed to expand their networks throughout territories, and the giants in these industries grew from combinations or mergers of small organizations employing parallel technologies. The expansion of the Bell Telephone System into a national network, despite the presence of a swarm of small "dependent independents," is also clear. The growth of branch banking where this is legally permissible is further evidence of the push to reduce contingencies, for the local bank is often constrained by a uniformity of economic fortunes in an undiversified territory, while a banking system expanding through many local communities enjoys a diversity that reduces the possibility of disaster. Bank mergers, especially where branch banking is curtailed, further illustrates this.

The insurance firm must find enough poolers of risk to avoid the possibility of any one loss destroying the coverage of others. Within a given risk category, the insurance organization must achieve large numbers of customers or else become dependent on other insurance organizations through reinsurance.

Sears, Roebuck, whose original success came by saturating rural territories via mail orders and deliveries, expanded still further as the population moved into urban areas where consumers were not dependent on catalogue shopping, by blanketing those areas with retail outlets (Chandler, 1962).

Proposition 4.1c: Organizations employing intensive technologies, and subject to rationality norms seek to expand their domains by incorporating the object worked on.

When the intensive application of collected, specialized capacities represents a change in rather than merely a service to the client, the activity of the client himself becomes an important contingency for the organization. We would expect, therefore, that organizations operating intensively on the client seek to place their boundaries around that client; these have been termed "inducting organizations" (Bidwell and Vreeland, 1963). The university incorporates its clients as student members, subject not only to the teaching-learning process and activities of the organization but to its discipline and constraints on other matters. The general hospital may operate an outpatient service, but its toughest cases are admitted for round-the-clock participation inside the organization and are expected to abide by hospital norms and regulations to the extent permitted by their condition.

In both cases the organization incorporates its clients on a temporary basis to reduce the possibility of contamination of the client by outside factors which might reduce or negate the effectiveness of the organization's efforts.

Where the intended change in the client is extreme, the placing of boundaries around the client is virtually -complete and converts the organization into what Goffman (1957) has termed a *total institution*— "a place of residence and work where a large number of like-situation individuals, cut off from a wider society for an appreciable period of time, together lead an enclosed, formally administered round of life."

In their early history, general hospitals in the United States were custodial institutions for the dying poor; they were transformed into therapeutic organizations by the gradual emergence of effective medical technology until they were finally seen, by those wealthy who were determined to live, as more effective sites for medical practice than the home. But they were also seen by medical practitioners as better sites for the practice of medicine, because they provided not only equipment and technicians, but also twenty-four-hour-a-day control of the environment to standards believed most conducive to patient health or recovery (Lentz, 1957). Perhaps the most dramatic attempt to cash in on the around-the-clock controlled environment of the human object is in those mental hospitals which concentrate on milieu therapy (Jones, 1953; Stanton and Schwartz, 1954). Here the organization is not content to neutralize the environment in standard ways, but actively seeks to use the interaction of the patient with that environment for therapeutic purposes.

When the output of the intensive technology calls for less drastic changes in the client, the placing of boundaries around that client is less complete, although the tendency remains clear. In the construction industry, for example, the contractor and the customer establish a relationship which has the effect of placing the customer in the project's administrative apparatus; and if the customer is an organization rather than an individual, the customer's agent may be a full-time liaison member of the project. Similarly, in the construction of custom, heavy industrial equipment, the customer may detail specialists to represent him within the producing organization during construction. During the installation and trial periods, the producing organization may detail its specialists to be members of the consuming organization. Industrial firms providing intensive-technology products to the military and space agencies employ technical representatives whose bases of operations are in the consuming organizations, and whose daily activities are geared more directly to the host organizations which employ them.

BALANCING OF COMPONENTS

We have indicated one important reason why complex organizations grow—to incorporate what otherwise would be serious contingencies. The organization which extends its boundaries to incorporate the sources of contingencies often finds that it has acquired capacity in excess of that called for by its major mission. The problem of balance emerges (Boulding, 1953).

Almost inevitably, growth of the type discussed above multiplies the components of the organization. And although we have for simplicity purposes treated organizations as if they employed only one type of core technology, we must recognize that expanded organizations may employ combinations of them. Thus the Bell Telephone System employs the mediating technology, saturating an extremely large territory, but also employs the long-linked technology in the production and installation of its own equipment, since that technology remains within a fairly narrow band. On such occasions as special events, the Bell system may also employ the intensive technology.

Expansion which entails combinations of core technologies further multiplies organizational components.

The multiple-component organization inevitably faces problems of balancing the capacities of its components. The balancing problem is most widely known within the technical cores of long-linked technologies, but it is perhaps even more significant when we compare the capacities of overall components in the total organization rather than merely comparing the capacities of individual machines or man-machine stations within a shop or department.

The problem arises essentially because capacities are not necessarily *continuously divisible*. The organization which is vertically integrated, for example, may contain greater capacity at some production stages than at others. This may occur because integration has proceeded through acquisition or merger of other organizations which had not been geared to the same rate of operations, but the primary reason for balancing problems lies in the technology and the task environment. Some resources come only in certain sizes. In order to have a machine which will make the desired 50 units per time period, it may be necessary to obtain one which will make 200. In order to offer one course each term in sociology, the university may have to acquire a full-time sociologist.

Frequently the problem is posed not in an all-or-nothing form but as one of *economy of scale*, another concept of central importance in the discipline of economics, but of realistic importance to all types of complex organizations. The economy-of-scale principle is best known in connection with problems internal to manufacturing, technical-core activities. But as Knauth (1956) shows, the advantages of bigness in industry include easier, less expensive financing; more numerous, highly trained intellects to attack trouble spots; sustained research; and more accurately tailored and adaptable marketing systems. Thus even though capacities may be continuously divisible, their incorporation on a small scale may not be feasible. This becomes especially clear when organizations grow by extending domains to new populations or territories. In order to provide telephone service to two Podunk subscribers, it may be necessary to install not only the equipment installed for a new subscriber in Manhattan, but also the central office equipment, lines, and service facilities suitable for providing service to Podunk's entire population.

Even more significant, perhaps, is the fact that capacity is not simply a matter of the present. The resources incorporated in a capacity are themselves more or less enduring, more or less mobile, more or less disposable. The costs of acquiring resources are often so great that the organization subjected to rationality norms must make commitments to future use of those resources. Certainly components which have long lives

(1) what kind of
orgs build
platforms/systems?

Simplicity of mobile web tech allows for easy competitors (no org challenges) BUT also increased scaling implications (No lo-memory of scaling)

and call for large investments may be mobile in the sense that one organization can divest itself of these to another organization. Nevertheless, any technology complicated enough to require a complex organization usually calls for a combination of components of varying capacities, varying lengths of usefulness, varying costs, and varying ease of divestment.

It is not unusual, therefore, for complex organizations of all types to acquire capacities which do not balance.

Proposition 4.2: Multicomponent organizations subject to rationality norms will seek to grow until the least-reducible component is approximately fully occupied.

From this proposition, for example, we would expect the manufacturing organization which in integrating forward has acquired distributive capacity greater than its manufacturing output, to then increase output. But this example immediately implies a question about the ability or willingness of the task environment to absorb such increased output. Under rationality norms, there must be some balance not only of component capacities but also between output and demand.

One major device for balancing the capacities of the organization against demand is to stimulate demand to the point where it equals capacity, but balancing technological capacity against demand does not automatically guarantee that output channels will be fully utilized. Another possibility is to equate output-channel capacity with demand, but this does not guarantee that the core technology will be fully employed. Even if such devices were adequate to balance the several component capacities and demand, the balance is not likely to be a stable one, for demand can and does change as a result of factors which no organization can forestall, even if it can forecast them. Moreover, advances in the technical process itself may result in increased capacity, thereby upsetting the balance.

Arch. which are fundamentally single-task (mobile) are prone to fragile deman changes

Proposition 4.3: Organizations with capacity in excess of what the task environment supports will seek to enlarge their domains.

Excess capacity has frequently occurred among integrated industrial organizations, not only to individual firms but to entire industries from time to time: oil, power machinery, agricultural products, electrical and electronics, and so on (Chandler, 1962). It has also plagued railroads, telegraph firms, and such organizations as the National Foundation (Sills, 1957). A widespread response to excess capacity has been the redesign of the organization by *diversification,* the development of new products

(track change in top- to app spttes)

or services. Since we have argued that domain is defined, in part, by the services or products offered, diversification by definition involves enlargement of domain if not the development of multiple domains.

Perhaps the simplest form of diversification springs from excess technological capacity and results in new products to which that capacity is closely allied and easily adapted. When depression reduced demand for gasoline, for example, the major oil firms, using the same refining processes, equipment, and raw materials, developed other refined products—such as household heating oil, diesel oil for railroads and utility firms, and high-octane gasoline for aircraft (Chandler, 1962).

A somewhat more drastic form of diversification springs from excess capacity in output channels and takes the form of products which are from quite different technologies but associated with original products so far as the demand environment is concerned. Thus Pittsburgh Plate Glass, to make fuller use of its marketing resources, developed a line of paints, brushes, and related items that could be sold through the same channels as window and plate glass (Chandler, 1962). Insurance companies originally offering a single line, such as fire insurance, developed into multiple-line companies offering a variety of types of insurance through the same marketing channels.

On other occasions, diversification springs from a newly emergent demand to which either technology or output-channel capacity can be readily converted. Thus Schenley distilleries were prepared to diversify into antibiotics when the demand emerged because of Schenley's mastery of and long experience with fermentation processes (Penrose, 1959).

Occasionally diversification springs from the very success of an organization in completely settling the demand it originally set out to meet; for example, the National Foundation for Infantile Paralysis became the National Foundation and entered several new disease domains as it became apparent that polio was on the verge of disappearing. Although the Townsend movement (Messinger, 1955) and the WCTU (Gusfield, 1955) apparently failed to diversify in the face of declining demand, the YMCA has effectively offered new services appealing to new categories of the population throughout its history (Zald and Denton, 1963).

Diversification is most noticeable among business organizations, perhaps because it is often accomplished through widely publicized acquisitions or mergers of well-known firms. But the diversification process is found in other types of organizations as well.

American universities in the last half-century have proliferated with a great variety of new departments, institutes, and schools. In some cases these simply reflect the intensification of knowledge which results in new disciplines, and are structural reactions to unwieldy categories of knowledge. Political science has emerged out of the field of history and is now regarded as something different and separable. This type of splintering springs from developments in the university's technology rather than from attempts to capture new markets; although once the process begins, other universities may follow in order to retain their drawing power. But the proliferation of institutes and schools in business administration, industrial and labor relations, international relations, public affairs and administration, etc, represents diversification to appeal to new elements of the task environment. These schools and institutes rest on commitments of resources in new combinations, appealing to new sources of support in order to more productively employ resources.

Hospitals may open new outpatient clinics or establish new services —for example, in nervous diseases—to round out utilization of services (Perrow, 1961b); and welfare organizations may extend domains to new clientele with new services.

Some Limitations

While it has been easy to cite examples fitting the above propositions, it would not be difficult to find examples of organizations which have not taken the steps indicated and apparently have not even sought to take them. Unless we can identify the conditions under which our propositions do hold, they have little merit.

To the student of American organizations, probably the most striking feature is the constraint exercised on organizations by governments, especially in the economic sector. National legislation has had the effect of reducing "combinations in restraint of trade," and on occasion, legal action under such legislation has sought to undo actions which had been consistent with our hypotheses. Governmental intervention to constrain the actions of organizations does not destroy our propositions; indeed, the growth of such legislation indicates that the kinds of tendencies we are dealing with are real and strong. But in addition to governmental constraints, there are other conditions that limit the application of our propositions.

No matter how crucial a capacity or activity, the organization need not attempt to incorporate it if the organization can be certain of its availability, when needed, on reasonable terms. Thus the organization with power relative to another which controls a needed activity need not formally incorporate that activity (Props. 3.1, 3.2, 3.3).

Lack of power to achieve the designs suggested above could obviously prevent the indicated changes. The creation or acquisition of units in vertical integration or through expansion may require considerable resources, sometimes more than an organization can mobilize. Saturation of existing markets can come incrementally, through addition of facilities for purchasing, introducing better service, or increasing quantity or varieties of offerings. But territorial expansion is a much more demanding move. It means entering a territory where facilities are lacking or insufficient, and entails investment in personnel, warehouses, supplies, advertising, displays, demonstrations, and perhaps in service facilities (Knauth, 1956). The decision to place boundaries around clients requires a commitment to a host of supporting facilities and services which may be too costly. Thus the metropolitan-commuter university may be tempted to become a residential university (reducing the impact of noneducational forces on students), but may find the provision of dormitories, dining halls, etc., extremely costly.

The norm of rationality may be subordinated to other norms, thus negating the patterns suggested in our propositions. The urban university may commit itself not to providing the best possible education but to providing education to commuter, part-time students. The business firm which has been a family-controlled enterprise may place higher priority on family control than on rationality, and resist growing beyond the family's ability to control. At the point where our propositions would take effect, the required resources might necessitate "going public" by selling stock to outsiders; a commitment to family control can prevent this (Landes, 1951).

Finally, the design of an organization which, in hindsight, appears logical and effective may be slow to emerge or may not emerge at all because the administrative process must operate without the benefit of hindsight. To arrive at our simple propositions we have sought to abstract a few significant variables from already-distilled sources. But the administrative processes operate within a detailed environment which contains masses of ambiguous and sometimes contradictory data. The process of refining these crude data into a decision to redesign an organization may be slow and halting (Dale, 1960; Chandler, 1962).

RECAPITULATION

Although complex organizations cannot be self-sufficient, they may have options on what things to do for themselves and what things to depend on from others. Under norms of rationality (Prop. 4.1), organizations seek to place their boundaries around those activities which if left to the task environment would be crucial contingencies. Because different types of technologies pose different kinds of crucial contingencies, we expect the direction of this boundary expansion to be patterned according to the kind of core technologies used in the organization.

The acquisition of components to handle otherwise crucial contingencies frequently forces organizations to acquire components of unequal capacities, and this raises balancing problems. We expect organizations subject to rationality norms (Prop. 4.2) to seek to grow until the least-reducible component is approximately fully occupied. If necessary in order to achieve this state (Prop. 4.3), organizations with excess capacity will seek to enlarge their domains.

Although governmental constraints or lack of power or administrative insight may prevent these propositions from operating universally, we believe that the technological pressures toward reduction of uncertainty, coupled with the uncertainties and contingencies inherent in environment, generate pressures for organizations to grow, and that the direction of growth is not random but is guided by the nature of the technology and of the task environment.

If organizations vary in design, they must also vary in structure, and we turn to this possibility in the following chapter.

are at least forces that constrain the design space? *technology and structure*

The major components of a complex organization are determined by the design of that organization. Invariably these major components are further segmented, or departmentalized, and connections are established within and between departments. It is this internal differentiation and patterning of relationships that we will refer to as *structure*. This chapter will focus on the impact of technological requirements on structure. The phenomena we will be dealing with therefore are to be found in those components of an organization which are most protected from environmental influences, the technical core. (In the following chapter we will consider environmental influences on structure, and the net effects of both technical and environmental factors.)

In considering structure we are involved with a sociotechnical system (Trist and Banforth, 1951), a system containing both human and non-human resources or facilities. For present purposes, however, the focus will be on differentiation and linkages of the individuals in the organization; that is, on the social structure. The technical parts of the system will not be ignored, however, for they provide a major orientation for the social structure.

But why have structure? There are both instrumental and economic reasons, and since we have argued earlier (Chapter 2) that the instrumental question is prior to that of efficiency, it may be helpful to consider a complex organization which scores well on tests of instrumental rationality but not on efficiency. This may help pinpoint the instrumental reasons for structure and also isolate those aspects of structure whose absence accounts for inefficiency.

The Synthetic Organization

Consider the *ad hoc* organization which usually emerges to overcome the effects of large-scale natural disasters in communities (at least in modern industrialized societies). We have labeled this the *synthetic organization* (Thompson and Hawkes, 1962).

When a major disaster strikes a community, the resources designed or earmarked for disaster recovery are in short supply. In a surprisingly short time and with little of the random, aimless behavior sometimes attributed to disasters, resources designed for other purposes are disengaged from their normal employment and adapted to disaster-recovery activities. This applies both to human and nonhuman resources.

Initial efforts at disaster recovery occur whenever resources and an obvious need or use for them occur simultaneously. At this point there is not a highly organized effort; instead there are a series of efforts, each isolated from the others. In a relatively short time, usually, two things happen to change this situation and bring about a synthetic organization: (1) uncommitted resources arrive, with those who possess them seeking places to use them, and (2) information regarding need for additional resources begins to circulate. When knowledge of need and resources coincide at a point in space, the *headquarters* of the synthetic organization has been established. Such headquarters only occasionally emerge around previously designated officers, indicating that their power rests not on authority in any formal sense but upon scarce capacity to coordinate. Only occasionally does this power fall to previously designated officers; rather, authority to coordinate the use of resources is attributed to—forced upon—the individual or group which by happenstance is at the crossroads of the two kinds of necessary information, resource availability and need.

The synthetic organizations involved in disaster-recovery activities are *ad hoc* organizations and usually dissolve rather rapidly. But when normal organizations are immobilized or overtaxed by sudden disaster, the synthetic organization rapidly develops structure to the point where coordinated action is instrumentally rational, with resources deployed and employed in complementary ways toward the overriding objective. Some individuals or component groups may have had training in preparation for disasters, but the synthetic organization emerges without the benefit of planning or blueprints, prior designations of authority, or formal authority to enforce its rules or decisions. What it does have, compared with normal organizations, is (1) consensus among participants about the state of affairs to be achieved and (2) great freedom to acquire and deploy resources, since the normal institutions of authority, property, and contract are not operating. Men and women may simply leave their places of work without permission or notice. Property rights may be waived or ignored as tools and equipment are pressed into service. Contractual arrangements for restitution of commandeered facilities may be forgotten—until later.

We have said that such organizations usually are instrumentally rational; the job gets done. But they are not efficient; some of the resources are not employed to their capacity, and some are employed at cross purposes. Why? Perhaps the overriding reason is that the synthetic organization must simultaneously establish its structure and carry on operations. Under conditions of great uncertainty, it must learn the nature and extent of the overall problem to be solved and the nature and location of relevant resources. At the same time it must assemble and interrelate the components, and it must do all this without benefit of established rules or commonly known channels of communication. The synthetic organization cannot take inventory before swinging into action. As information mounts, task priorities change; meanwhile resources have been committed to other tasks which a moment earlier appeared to have top priority.

The synthetic organization for disaster recovery is inefficient by technological or economic standards because it must order the actions of its components in a situation of interdependence and in the face of uncertainty as to where and how that interdependence exists. It can be presumed that efficiency would be higher if the synthetic-organization headquarters knew in advance either the extent of the problem to be solved or the full array of resources available to it, and that maximum efficiency would be achieved if both were known in advance. Under those conditions it could plan, establish relevant rules, and provide communication channels among its departments.

Our basic assumption is that structure is a fundamental vehicle by which organizations achieve bounded rationality (Simon, 1957b). By delimiting responsibilities, control over resources, and other matters, organizations provide their participating members with boundaries within which efficiency may be a reasonable expectation. But if structure affords numerous spheres of bounded rationality, it must also facilitate the *coordinated* action of those *interdependent* elements. It appears that if we wish to understand organization structure, we must consider what is meant by interdependence and by coordination, and we must consider various types of these.

INTERNAL INTERDEPENDENCE

Both the natural-system and rational models of complex organizations assume interdependence of organizational parts, the rational model being somewhat more specific about the location of interdependence and somewhat more circumscribed about the nature of the interdependence assumed.

To assume that an organization is composed of interdependent parts is not necessarily to say that each part is dependent on, and supports, every other part in any direct way. The Tuscaloosa branch of an organization may not interact at all with the Oshkosh branch, and neither may have contact with the Kokomo branch. Yet they may be interdependent in the sense that unless each performs adequately, the total organization is jeopardized; failure of any one can threaten the whole and thus the other parts. We can describe this situation as one in which each part renders a discrete contribution to the whole and each is supported by the whole. We will call this *pooled interdependence.*

Interdependence may also take a serial form, with the Keokuk plant producing parts which become inputs for the Tucumcari assembly operation. Here both make contributions to and are sustained by the whole organization, and so there is a pooled aspect to their interdependence. But, in addition, direct interdependence can be pinpointed between them, and the order of that interdependence can be specified. Keokuk must act properly before Tucumcari can act; and unless Tucumcari acts, Keokuk cannot solve its output problem. We will refer to this as *sequential interdependence,* and note that it is not symmetrical.

A third form of interdependence can be labeled *reciprocal,* referring to the situation in which the outputs of each become inputs for the others. This is illustrated by the airline which contains both operations and maintenance units. The production of the maintenance unit is an input for operations, in the form of a serviceable aircraft; and the product (or by-product) of operations is an input for maintenance, in the form of an aircraft needing maintenance. Under conditions of reciprocal interdependence, each unit involved is penetrated by the other. There is, of course, a pooled aspect to this, and there is also a serial aspect since the aircraft in question is used by one, then by the other, and again by the first. But the distinguishing aspect is the reciprocity of the interdependence, with each unit posing contingency for the other.

In the illustrations advanced above—and in reality, we believe—the types of interdependence form a Guttman-type scale (Stouffer et al., 1950): all organizations have pooled interdependence; more complicated organizations have sequential as well as pooled; and the most complex have reciprocal, sequential, and pooled. Knowing that an organization contains reciprocal interdependence automatically tells us that it also contains sequential and pooled interdependence. Knowing that an organization contains sequential interdependence tells us that it also contains the pooled type. Knowing that an organization contains pooled interdependence, however, does not tell us whether it has the others.

In the order introduced, the three types of interdependence are increasingly difficult to coordinate because they contain increasing degrees of contingency. With pooled interdependence, action in each position can proceed without regard to action in other positions so long as the overall organization remains viable. With sequential interdependence, however, each position in the set must be readjusted if any one of them acts improperly or fails to meet expectations. There is always an element of potential contingency with sequential interdependence. With reciprocal interdependence, contingency is not merely potential, for the actions of each position in the set must be adjusted to the actions of one or more others in the set.

Because the three types of interdependence are, in the order indicated, more difficult to coordinate, we will say that they are more costly to coordinate, noting that measurement of such costs is far from perfect.

COORDINATION

In a situation of interdependence, concerted action comes about through coordination; and if there are different types of interdependence, we would expect to find different devices for achieving coordination. The work of March and Simon (1958) is particularly useful for this purpose, although we will want to tamper with their labels.

Under some conditions coordination may be achieved by *standardization*. This involves the establishment of routines or rules which constrain action of each unit or position into paths consistent with those taken by others in the interdependent relationship. An important assumption in coordination by standardization is that the set of rules be internally consistent, and this requires that the situations to which they apply be relatively stable, repetitive, and few enough to permit matching of situations with appropriate rules.

In the March and Simon formulation, *coordination by plan* involves the establishment of schedules for the interdependent units by which their actions may then be governed. Coordination by plan does not require the same high degree of stability and routinization that are required for coordination by standardization, and therefore is more appropriate for more dynamic situations, especially when a changing task environment impinges on the organization.

A third form can be called *coordination by mutual adjustment,* and involves the transmission of new information during the process of action. (In March and Simon terms, this is "coordination by feedback," but the term "feedback" has gathered a connotation of super/subordination which unduly restricts it for our purposes. Coordination by mutual adjustment may involve communication across hierarchical lines, but it cannot be assumed that it necessarily does.) The more variable and unpredictable the situation, March and Simon observe, the greater the reliance on coordination by mutual adjustment.

Now we can make two observations about interdependence and coordination which are crucial to our examination of structure:

First, there are distinct parallels between the three types of interdependence and the three types of coordination. With pooled interdependence, coordination by standardization is appropriate; with sequential interdependence, coordination by plan is appropriate; and with reciprocal interdependence, coordination by mutual adjustment is called for.

Second, the three types of coordination, in the order introduced above, place increasingly heavy burdens on communication and decision. Standardization requires less frequent decisions and a smaller volume of communication during a specific period of operations than does planning, and planning calls for less decision and communication activity than does mutual adjustment. There are very real costs involved in coordination.

DEPARTMENTALIZATION

Luther Gulick, one of the pioneers of the administrative management school, noted that positions or components of organizations could be grouped, or separated, on four different bases: (1) common purpose or contribution to the larger organization, (2) common processes, (3) a particular clientele, or (4) a particular geographic area (Gulick and Urwick, 1937). These are, in brief, alternative ways of *homogenizing* positions or components. The difficulty with this scheme, and the difficulties real-life organizations have in choosing methods of grouping, lies in the fact that positions or components of complex organizations are not unidimensional. Homogenizing them on one dimension does not homogenize them on all dimensions. As Simon (1957a) has observed, placing school health activities in the department of education relates those activities to other educational efforts, but prevents the assignment of school health activities to a health department where they would be related to other medical activities.

The fact is that complex organizations meet all four problems indicated by Gulick. Their components serve different purposes for the larger organization, they employ several processes, they frequently serve more than one clientele, and for the most part they are geographically extended. The question is not which criterion to use for grouping, but rather in which *priority* are the several criteria to be exercised. That priority, we suggest, is determined by the nature and location of interdependency, which is a function of both technology and task environment (Miller, 1959).

The question of the grouping of positions can be stated as a matter of arranging for some positions to be *tangent* to one another. Shall position A be placed tangent to position B or to position H? Should positions A, B, and H all be tangent to one another, or is it imperative that position H be placed tangent to position X, which requires that it be removed from direct linkage with positions A and B?

Proposition 5.1: Under norms of rationality, organizations group positions to minimize coordination costs.

We have argued that coordination by mutual adjustment is more costly, involving greater decision and communication burdens, than coordination by plan, which in turn is more costly than coordination by standardization. We would therefore expect first priority to be given to grouping in such a way as to minimize the more costly forms of coordination.

Proposition 5.1a: Organizations seek to place reciprocally interdependent positions tangent to one another, in a common group which is (*a*) local and (*b*) conditionally autonomous.

There is nothing startling about the fact that when technology calls for action by crews or teams, the necessary positions are grouped into crews or teams; this is commonplace at the grass roots, or lowest levels, of complex organizations. A more subtle aspect, however, is the localization of such groups. Because coordination by mutual adjustment is expensive, and its costs increase as the number of positions involved increases, we would expect organizations facing reciprocal interdependence to fashion the smallest possible groups. (Note that we are not saying this will apply throughout organizations, but in those sectors of organizations where reciprocal interdependence is mandatory.)

Now if A, B, and C are reciprocally interdependent members of a team or crew and interact only among themselves, coordination is less troublesome than if one or more of the members were also reciprocally interdependent with X, or Y, or Z. Automony of the group as such facilitates coordination by mutual adjustment, but we must recognize that autonomy is modified; the fully autonomous unit would not be or remain a part of the organization. Thus we have used the term *conditionally autonomous,* and we would argue that organizations seek to group reciprocally interdependent positions into local units, autonomous within the constraints established by plans and standardization.

Proposition 5.1b: In the absence of reciprocal interdependence, organizations subject to rationality norms seek to place sequentially interdependent positions tangent to one another, in a common group which is (*a*) localized and (*b*) conditionally autonomous.

The costs of planning grow rapidly as the number of variables increases and as the lines of communication lengthen. The costs of planning are therefore minimized when done in small units rather than large ones, and we would expect organizations to lodge the planning chore in the smallest possible cluster of serially interdependent positions.

Proposition 5.1c: In the absence of reciprocal and sequential interdependence, organizations subject to norms of rationality seek to group positions homogeneously to facilitate coordination by standardization.

By definition a complex organization contains differentiation of parts, hence heterogeneity. But to the extent that technological requirements permit and environmental fluctuations can be warded off (a major gain from Proposition 2.1), the grouping of positions performing similar processes permits coordination to be handled in the least costly manner. Homogeneity facilitates coordination because one set of rules applies to all positions in the group; and when changes in rules are necessary, one set of changes applies to all.

HIERARCHY

Our argument can so far be summarized in the following form: The basic units are formed to handle reciprocal interdependence, if any. If there is none, then the basic units are shaped according to sequential interdependence, if any. If neither of the more complicated types of interdependence exists, the basic units are shaped according to common processes.

Problems arise, however, if the three types of interdependence form a Guttman-type scale, where all organizations have pooled interdependence; more complex organizations also have sequential interdependence, and the most complex have reciprocal interdependence in addition to the other two forms. If the basic groups are formed to deal satisfactorily with reciprocal interdependence, they still must deal with the other types. Moreover, it is not always possible to contain reciprocal interdependence within first-order groupings.

Proposition 5.2: When reciprocal interdependence cannot be confined to intragroup activities, organizations subject to rationality norms seek to link the groups involved into a second-order group, as localized and conditionally autonomous as possible.

On occasion, reciprocal interdependence is so extensive that to link all of the involved positions into one group would overtax communication mechanisms. When this occurs, organizations rank-order the interdependent positions in terms of the amount of contingency each poses for the others. Those with the greatest intercontingency form a group, and the resulting groups are then clustered into an overarching second-order group.

We have now introduced the first step in a *hierarchy*. It is unfortunate that this term has come to stand almost exclusively for degrees of highness or lowness, for this tends to hide the basic significance of hierarchy for complex organizations. Each level is not simply higher than the one below, but is a more inclusive *clustering*, or combination of interdependent groups, to handle those aspects of coordination which are beyond the scope of any of its components.

Chester Barnard (1938) noted that for every group in a complex organization there is one position which also "belongs" to another group, composed of representatives of other groups. It is our contention that the composition of each more inclusive group is determined by coordination requirements—by the locus of interdependence or contingency. The first rule for composition of this second-order combination is to dispose of reciprocal interdependence not adequately handled by the initial grouping of positions.

[Boulding (1964) has offered the interesting proposition that the hierarchical structure of organization can largely be interpreted as a device for the resolution of conflicts, with each grade of the hierarchy specializing in resolving the conflicts of the grade beneath it. This seems to parallel the argument advanced here, if we assume that the probability of conflict among positions or groups is directly proportional to their degree of interdependence.]

Proposition 5.3: After grouping units to minimize coordination by mutual adjustment, organizations under rationality norms seek to place sequentially interdependent groups tangent to one another, in a cluster which is localized and conditionally autonomous.

Again at the level of intergroup ties, as in the case of interposition ties, we are saying that after reciprocal interdependence has been solved by grouping, the criterion of sequential interdependence is employed.

Proposition 5.4: After grouping units to solve problems of reciprocal and sequential interdependence, organizations under norms of rationality seek to cluster groups into homogeneous units to facilitate coordination by standardization.

We would expect to find this criterion for higher-order clustering of groups only in relatively simple organizations. In the more complicated organizations, the criteria of reciprocal and sequential interdependence tend to exhaust the clustering possibilities before this third criterion can be exercised. In complex organizations, then, we would expect:

Proposition 5.4a: When higher-priority coordination requirements prevent the clustering of similar positions or groups, organizations seek to blanket homogeneous positions under rules which cut across group boundaries, and to blanket similar groups under rules which cross divisional lines.

We asserted that when dealing with coordination by mutual adjustment or by planning, organizations seek to localize interaction and to confine it to conditionally autonomous groups—to cluster positions and groups into the smallest possible inclusive units in order to minimize coordination costs. When coordinating via standardization, however, organizations seek to make rules pervasive in order to apply to the widest possible categories. Where grouping on the basis of common procedures is not feasible, organizations may still employ standardization by devising rules which apply to certain processes or categories of activity whenever and wherever these occur in the organization.

Proposition 5.4b: When organizations employ standardization which cuts across multiple groupings, they also develop liaison positions linking the several groups and the rule-making agency.

We find a variety of "staff" positions in complex organizations, many of which are intended as linkages between operating groups and standard-formulating centers. Illustrative are personnel or industrial relations specialists at intermediate levels of the hierarchy who presumably advise specialists of other types when personnel or industrial relations actions are involved. Similarly, accountants or controllers at intermediate levels are presumably expert counselors to those levels on matters pertaining to the accounting for action. In both cases, of course, the staff specialists are as likely to be as responsive to the rule-formulating centers as to the level they advise.

These liaison or staff positions are appropriate when the interdependence is of the pooled type, requiring the formulation, interpretation, and application of rules for standardization. They are less effective for other types of interdependence, and complex organizations typically employ other devices to deal with interdependence which spills over or is not contained by the usual formal structure.

Proposition 5.4c: Organizations with sequential interdependence not contained by departmentalization rely on committees to accomplish the remaining coordination.

Proposition 5.4d: Organizations with reciprocal interdependence not contained by departmentalization rely on task-force or project groupings to accomplish the remaining coordination.

AN ILLUSTRATION

To see these propositions crystallized in action, we need an example of an organization (or complex suborganization) which is relatively free of contaminating contingencies from the environment. The medium bomb wing of the Strategic Air Command of the United States Air Force, when operating B-50 manned aircraft, affords such an example (Thompson, 1953). To a greater extent than in most complex organizations, environmental contingencies were removed during peacetime. The bomb wing was embedded in a relatively friendly environment composed of other Air Force units whose mission was to support it. During peacetime operations the absence of an enemy left as the major environmental contingencies the weather and higher headquarters, which from the wing's level often appeared to act capriciously.

Most of the inputs required by the wing were extensively buffered by other air force units. Manpower was recruited, trained, and indoctrinated; equipment and supplies were procured and delivered; buildings and other facilities were erected and maintained—all by units subject to the same ultimate authority. This is not to maintain that such other units were necessarily subservient to the wing, for they were resources to a number of wings, and this raised problems in resource allocation among wings; but it does suggest that environmental hostility was minimized compared with many organizations embedded in task environments composed of multiple sovereign organizations.

In this highly protected organization, structure primarily reflected technological contingencies.

The ultimate effectiveness of the bomb wing depended on the co-ordinated action of the ten-man crew which operated the aircraft and its equipment. Even in peacetime the variety of unpredictable problems that could arise was large, and training missions were designed to prepare for the still greater contingencies that would arise from enemy action during wartime operations. Since the aircraft and its equipment could only be operated effectively by a ten-man team of specialists, and since each had to adjust his actions to the actions of others, the bomb wing ultimately depended on the mutual adjustment of the members of this team. The air crew, then, became the basic grass-roots group in the wing's structure (Prop. 5.1a), and its significance is demonstrated by the high priority given to crew integrity.

Under crucial conditions, the mutual adjustment of crew activities had to be almost instantaneous; hence communication had to be rapid, direct, and unambiguous. Regular operation of the crew as a team permitted individuals to learn each other's idiosyncrasies and action habits, thus facilitating mutual adjustment. Holding the same ten individuals together as one team—crew integrity—was a high-priority policy in medium bomb wings.

Crews as units were also interdependent with other groups. The aircraft, for example, was alternately flown and maintained, and maintenance was such an important aspect of crew operations that first-echelon maintenance teams were located tangent to crews. Since incorporation of maintenance teams into air crews would have unduly expanded air crews beyond the boundaries of their reciprocal contingencies, air crews and first-echelon maintenance teams were separate groupings, but their tangency was assured by incorporating both into a second-level grouping known as the *bomb squadron* (Prop. 5.2). The squadron provided a means of dealing with sequential interdependence, not only between air crews and maintenance teams, but also in scheduling crews and available aircraft for flying missions and for other types of ground training.

From time to time, various types of specialized maintenance were required. Aircraft periodically required major inspections, and this was the responsibility of a specialized grouping known as the *periodic maintenance squadron*. Armament and electronic equipment on the aircraft also required maintenance, repair, or replacement, and this was the responsibility of still another specialized group known as the *armament and electronic maintenance squadron*. Finally, such major problems as engine changes and overhauls or fuselage repairs called for a different set of specialized skills, and these were grouped in a field maintenance squadron.

Because each of the specialized maintenance squadrons was a grouping to deal with only a part of the aircraft maintenance technology, they were placed in a third-order grouping (Prop. 5.2) which lacked a name but nevertheless was recognized by all concerned as headed by a director of material and his assistant, a maintenance control officer. The technology of maintenance precluded assignment of these activities to air crews or even to squadrons. One maintenance technology could, however, serve three flying squadrons, and the wing was composed essentially of a single maintenance system (internally differentiated) and three (identical) flying squadrons. To lump the three flying squadrons into one would have violated the need for localization of coordination (Prop. 5.1a), but with three identical squadrons seeking the services of a single maintenance system, scheduling had to be accomplished at a higher-order level. Hence a third-order grouping, headed by a director of operations, was provided, and served as a unit to establish sequential coordination of all flying groups with all maintenance groups (Prop. 5.3).

Finally, all units within the wing were subjected to common rules for utilization of personnel and for measuring and reporting performance.

Thus at the overarching wing-headquarters level there was a director of personnel and a comptroller, and in each squadron there were counterparts for these (Prop. 5.4*b*). e

For other necessary functions, including food, medical, police, and motor pool services, the degree of contingency was considerably reduced; and such activities, while located on the base, were clustered into an air base group separate from the wing but clustered together with the wing into the division.

At the time of this study (1952) of bomb wings, the Air Force was struggling with an ambivalence stemming from its changing technology and its slower-to-change traditions. According to tradition, the directors of operations and of material were staff aides to the wing commander and as such gave advice to squadron commanders. The technology, however, placed considerable contingency between the maintenance and the operations (flying) systems, which could not be contained within crews or squadrons, and whose solution could only take place between the systems themselves. The technology required that sequential coordination take place at the level of the two directors, and frequently through a coordinating committee (Prop. 5.4*c*) composed of those directors, the six squadron commanders, and the wing commander. If coordination was to be effective at the directors' level, it required that they have power to commit the resources of their respective systems, which in fact they did, regardless of tradition (Thompson, 1956).

One case, deliberately selected to be atypical, does not test a set of propositions, but the bomb wing does serve to illustrate in a more concrete sense the argument advanced in this chapter.

RECAPITULATION

There appear to be three types of interdependence stemming from technological requirements within organizations. Each has an appropriate method of coordination. It is the task of structure to facilitate the exercise of the appropriate coordinating processes. Pooled, or generalized, interdependence is coordinated by standardization, and is least costly in terms of communication and decision effort. Sequential interdependence is coordinated by planning and is intermediate in effort required. Reciprocal interdependence is coordinated by mutual adjustment and is most demanding of communication and decision effort.

Under norms of rationality, organizations group positions to minimize coordination costs (Prop. 5.1), localizing and making conditionally autonomous, first (Prop. 5.1a) reciprocally interdependent positions, then (Prop. 5.1b) sequentially interdependent ones, and finally (Prop. 5.1c) grouping positions homogeneously to facilitate standardization.

Because first groupings do not entirely handle interdependence, organizations link the groups involved (Props. 5.2, 5.3, and 5.4) into higher-order groups, thus introducing hierarchy. When interdependence is not contained by such departmental and divisional arrangements, organizations assign remaining problems of coordination to committees or to task-force or project teams.

But organizational structure must reflect interdependence of the organization and its environment, as well as its technology. We turn now to consideration of the influences of environment on organization structure.

6

organizational rationality and structure

In discussing technology and structure, we argued that structural divisions were established to delimit coordinative complexity. We predicted that positions and groups of positions would be clustered in a manner calculated to handle the most critical aspects of their interdependence. We assumed that the technology set the constraints around which the organization manipulated its variables, and that technical rationality is maximized when the variables are under complete control of the organization.

Because organizations are always embedded in larger systems of action (Chapter 2), some parts of the organization must be interdependent with organizations not subordinated to the organization, hence not subject to authoritative specification of permissible action. The crucial problem for boundary-spanning units of an organization, therefore, is not coordination (of variables under control) but *adjustment* to constraints and contingencies not controlled by the organization—to what the economist calls exogenous variables.

We have already suggested (Props. 2.2 and 2.3) that organizations subject to rationality norms seek to isolate their technical cores from environmental influences by establishing boundary-spanning units to buffer or level environmental fluctuations. These responsibilities help determine the structure of input and output units.

Varieties of Environmental Constraints

Those elements of the task environment to which the organization must adapt vary from organization to organization, and do not fit neatly with any of the typical distinctions among organizations.

Some governmental units, for example, must live only on the financial inputs provided by legislative units such as Congress or a city council, and have no option even to which nation, state, or city .they will attach themselves. But other governmental units do not find themselves so constrained regarding financial inputs. Many are empowered to raise capital funds through bond issues. Some may be self-supporting by charging fees for services; these may find, on the other hand, that their imperative is to deal with a specified clientele. This latter imperative may be equally true of the "private" public utility.

Prisons typically have no option regarding their clientele, and in this respect they may be compared with governmentally financed mental hospitals. Private mental hospitals, on the other hand, may be quite selective in their admissions policy (Belknap, 1956).

For a given organization, the nature of environmental constraints may change over time. Thus at an earlier period, the voluntary hospital was a charity institution for the dying; its location and often its clientele was specified by wealthy donors (Lentz, 1957). As the domain of the hospital was redefined by the development of medical technology and the rise of third-party payment arrangements such as Blue Cross, the voluntary hospital was no longer confined to a geographic site or clientele specified by a single wealthy donor. The textile mill at one time was obliged to locate at the source of water power, but the development of transmission lines and new sources of power freed the textile organization from this constraint.

Some organizations face constraints on the sources of raw material inputs; the extractive industries such as iron, petroleum, or lumber are examples. For others, raw material inputs may be easily available in any location or may be feasibly shipped and stored, but manpower inputs may constitute imperatives; various kinds of research organizations, for example, find they must locate where the relevant skills have been assembled.

It should be emphasized that the nature of an environmental constraint is not perfectly correlated with ownership of the organization, although Elling and Halebsky's (1961) study of community hospitals indicates that the source of sponsorship has significant impact on other aspects of their actions. We cannot say that because an organization is public, or government sponsored, it has a particular kind of environmental situation; nor that the private organization such as the business firm has another. Nor is there a one-to-one correlation between varieties of organizational constraints and the role in society of the organization. The impact of task environment is more subtle.

If these traditional modes of classifying organizations are inadequate for the purpose, on what basis may organizations and their environmental constraints be compared? Generally, we may say that organizations find their environmental constraints located in *geographic space* or in the *social composition* of their task environments. And if this is the case, we need ways of characterizing both dimensions.

Typically geographic space is described in terms of *distance* between points within it, but organizations usually measure this distance in terms of *costs of transportation* or *costs of communication*. The iron industry, for example, must bring together ore and coal, which are found at different points in geographic space. When the transporting of one or the other becomes easier or less costly, the firm's freedom to select from among various geographic locations becomes greater. Similarly, the development of electronic data-processing networks has the practical effect of reducing distance between points of the regionally scattered organization and thus permits centralization of decision making where heretofore localized units exercised local discretion in the interest of speedy response to local fluctuations.

There are fewer conventions with regard to the description and measurement of the social composition of environments. What we need are ways of differentiating among the kinds of social environments faced by complex organizations—the individual members, aggregates of individuals, and organizations which constitute task environments. A variety has been suggested recently. Task environments have been characterized by March and Simon (1958) as hostile or benign. Dill (1958) distinguished task environments as *homogeneous* or *heterogeneous, stable* or *rapidly shifting,* and *unified* or (by implication) *segmented.* Coleman (1957), in describing communities, considered organizational density.

For present purposes, dimensions dealing with degree of homogeneity and degree of stability seem most useful. In contrasting two firms, Dill (1958) found it helpful to characterize the task environments as (relatively) homogeneous or heterogeneous, indicating whether the social entities in it were, for organizationally relevant matters, similar to one another. In comparison with one serving a small city, the public school in an upper-middle-class suburb, for example, might enjoy a relatively homogeneous task environment with respect to the school expectations held by taxpayers and parents.

In Dill's study, the Alpha firm faced a relatively homogeneous environment, Beta, the heterogeneous one. Most of Alpha's customers ordered all four product lines, twice a year, and at the same time. The firm dealt with a single union, and virtually all of the external groups it dealt with were Norwegian. In contrast, Beta was active in a variety of quite distinct markets, dealt with three unions, and with suppliers and other groups in various parts of Europe. The task environment for both was pluralistic, but Dill makes the important point that not only did the firms differ in terms of the number of groups impinging on them, but that within each category (competitors, suppliers, customers, and regulatory agencies) the task environments were relatively homogeneous in one case and relatively heterogeneous in the other.

The social composition of task environments may also be characterized on a *stable-shifting* dimension. Dill noted, for example, that Alpha's market had changed relatively little in fifty years; although population had grown, the Norwegian family remained the only important customer. Products and means of distribution were basically the same. For Beta, however, markets that had existed when the firm was founded had grown in some cases and disappeared in others; only two of the major work activities were continuations of pre–World War I, the other eleven having resulted from the growth and diversification of the industries which used Beta's services, from rapid technological development of the equipment and processes in which Beta specialized, and from increases in the real prosperity of the Norweigan consumer. Although the shifts in Beta's case are described here in terms of what we have called domain, they undoubtedly reflect more day-to-day fluctuation for Beta than for Alpha.

Chandler (1962) has described the significance of day-to-day fluctuations in demand for the producers of perishable products like meat or fruit.

There are undoubtedly other dimensions of task environment which have a bearing on organization structure, but these two appear at this point to be quite crucial, and they have the important advantage that they can be applied to all types of organizations and task environments. We believe they will help us understand differences, at least gross distinctions, in organizational structures. Although both dimensions affect organizations simultaneously, we will first consider their consequences independently.

BOUNDARY-SPANNING STRUCTURES

If adjustment or adaptability is the hallmark of boundary-spanning components of organizations, we would expect that fact to be reflected in the number and nature of the units established to handle boundary-spanning matters. Generally, we would expect the complexity of the structure, the number and variety of units, to reflect the complexity of the environment. If organization structure is an important means of achieving bounded rationality, then the more difficult the environment, the more important it is to assign a small portion of it to one unit.

Proposition 6.1: Under norms of rationality, organizations facing heterogeneous task environments seek to identify homogeneous segments and establish structural units to deal with each.

This proposition is perhaps most dramatically illustrated by the organization which crosses national boundaries where environmental variations may be stark. Under these conditions, organizations tend to establish semiautonomous divisions based on region. Those organizations which dabble in foreign operations may simply have a foreign or nondomestic division; but when they become more deeply involved, they usually establish national or at least bloc entities (Dinerman, 1963; Chandler, 1962).

We need not cross cultural boundaries to see this proposition in action. Public school systems divide themselves into elementary and secondary schools, and only in rare cases are these ungraded internally. General hospitals establish separate units for obstetrics, contagious diseases, and surgical and outpatient services; mental hospitals often establish separate units for various types of disorders or severity of problems. Universities create undergraduate and graduate divisions. Public-assistance agencies may be divided into different units for dispensing unemployment compensation benefits, and aid to dependent children or the blind. Air conditioning manufacturers may create separate divisions to make and dispose of residential and commercial units. Transport firms create separate divisions for passenger and cargo traffic. Large multiproduct retail establishments, facing heterogeneity on the input side, create specialized buying units.

Proposition 6.2: Under norms of rationality, boundary-spanning components facing homogeneous segments of the task environment are further subdivided to match surveillance capacity with environmental action.

If the sheer volume of interaction between a boundary-spanning component and its task environment is great, even though homogeneous, we would expect the organization to find a means of subdividing that component. Often this may be done by area or region in geographic space, but it may be done by otherwise insignificant differences in social composition of the task environment, such as alphabet.

Surveillance capacity undoubtedly varies as a result of differences in data-collecting, transmitting, and processing devices; but at any specific time the available devices set conditions for the organization. The degree of stability of the task-environment segment is a further constraint.

Proposition 6.2a: The organization component facing a stable task environment will rely on rules to achieve its adaptation to that environment.

As in the case of coordination (Chapter 5), we believe that adaptation by rule is the least costly form, and therefore preferred by organizations which are under pressure to be efficient.

Proposition 6.2b: When the range of variation presented by the task-environment segment is known, the organization component will treat this as a constraint and adapt by standardizing sets of rules.

The organization may say that when the task environment behaves in manner A, respond according to rule 1; and when the task environment behaves in manner B, choose rule 2 (Blau, 1955; Francis and Stone, 1956). It is under these conditions that the bureaucratic procedures (Weber, 1947; Merton, 1957b) of categorizing events and selecting appropriate response rules become very important. But this manner of proceeding becomes unwieldy if the range of possible variations in task-environment behavior is great, for it entails a proliferation of sets of rules, and places heavy burdens on the organization's capacity to categorize—to judge which set of environmental constraints it faces at a particular point in time and space.

Proposition 6.2c: When the range of task-environment variations is large or unpredictable, the responsible organization component must achieve the necessary adaptation by monitoring that environment and planning responses, and this calls for localized units.

Now, the above propositions treated each dimension independently, and indeed we believe they are independent in their actions. Nevertheless, all organizations face task environments which are located simultaneously somewhere on the homogeneous-heterogeneous continuum and the stable-shifting continuum. We can consider the interaction of the two as follows:

	Stable	*Shifting*
Homo		
Hetero		

From our above propositions, we would expect the organization whose task environment is relatively homogeneous and relatively stable to be relatively simple in the structure of its boundary-spanning components. This organization would have few *functional divisions,* and if these were subdivided it would be into several similar departments or sections. This organization would rely primarily on standardized responses or rules for adaptation, the departments or sections would be rule-applying agencies, and administration would consist of rule enforcement.

For the organization facing a heterogeneous but stable task environment, we would expect a variety of functional divisions, each corresponding to a relatively homogeneous segment of the task environment, and each relying primarily on rules to achieve adaptation. These functional divisions might be further subdivided, on geographic or similar bases, into similar or uniform departments or sections, and would be rule-applying agencies.

When the task environment becomes dynamic rather than stable, new complications arise for the organization. Standardized response rules are inadequate, for the organization faces contingencies as well as constraints. It must determine when and how to act, and its cues must be taken from the task environment.

If the task environment is dynamic but relatively homogeneous, the boundary-spanning component need be differentiated or subdivided only to the extent that its capacity to monitor the environment would be over-extended. Since, by definition, the environment is otherwise homogeneous, we would expect sections or departments of this organization to be established by area in geographic space. Unlike the regional divisions established for the stable-environment case, however, the regional divisions for the dynamic environment will be less concerned with the application of rules than with the planning of responses to environmental changes. When the task environment is dynamic, the regional divisions will be *decentralized*.

Finally, we have the situation in which the task environment is both heterogeneous and dynamic. Here we would expect boundary-spanning units to be differentiated functionally to correspond to segments of the task environment, and each to operate on a decentralized basis to monitor and plan responses to fluctuations in its sector of the task environment.

The sum of our argument regarding the impact of task environment on the structure of boundary-spanning units may now be expressed. The more heterogeneous the task environment, the greater the constraints presented to the organization. The more dynamic the task environment, the greater the contingencies presented to the organization. Under either condition, the organization seeking to be rational must put boundaries around the amount and scope of adaptation necessary, and it does this by establishing structural units specialized to face a limited range of contingencies within a limited set of constraints. The more constraints and contingencies the organization faces, the more its boundary-spanning component will be segmented. This argument seems consistent with that of March and Simon, who "predict that process specialization will be carried furthest in stable environments, and that under rapidly changing circumstances specialization will be sacrificed to secure greater self-containment of separate programs" (p. 159).

THE ORGANIZATION AS A JOINT RESULT

The bases for grass-roots groups, and for successive combinations of groups into clusters, clusters into larger clusters, etc., eventually result in an overall structural pattern for the complex organization. This pattern varies widely from one organization to another; there is no one right way to structure all complex organizations. Yet the variations are not random. To a large extent they can be accounted for as attempts to solve the problems of concerted action under different conditions, especially conditions of technological and environmental constraints and contingencies. These conditions vary not only from one organization to another, but for a particular organization as (1) its task environment changes, (2) innovations modify technologies, or (3) the organization changes its domain and hence its task environment.

With so many reasons for diversity, what can we say in general about organizational structure? One thing seems obvious: size alone does not result in complexity. So long as an organization employs simple technologies and faces simple task environments, it can be large and still employ a relatively simple structure. Chandler (1962) found, for example, that copper companies were among the simplest industrial organizations in his study because they produced few types of products for a well-defined market, and their technical operations were quite routinized (p. 329).

On the other hand, an organization need not be large to be complex. Voluntary hospitals and universities, for example, tend toward the small end of the size scale, as organizations go, whether we measure size in terms of number of employees, size of budget, or cost of plant. Yet hospitals and universities are among the most complex of purposive organizations.

Since our reasoning posits coordinative and adaptive requirements as the bases of complexity, we would not expect the administrative load on organizations to be closely correlated with size. Hence it is not surprising to find studies which have attempted to correlate size and administrative overhead inconclusive, which they are (Anderson and Warkov, 1961; Starbuck, 1965; Hawley, Boland, and Boland, 1965; Haire, 1955).

One important variable in shaping organizations under conditions of complexity is the extent to which technical-core– and boundary-spanning components can be isolated from each other, the extent to which organizations can separate their rational-model requirements from their natural-system requirements. The comparison comes out clearly in Dill's study (1958). Frequently, he found, Beta's leaders could not deal with a customer without dealing at the same time with suppliers and other groups involved in the same project, and much of Beta's work was done on customers' premises. In Alpha, however, the components were less directly in interaction.

Proposition 6.3: When technical-core and boundary-spanning activities can be isolated from one another except for scheduling, organizations under norms of rationality will be centralized with an overarching layer composed of functional divisions.

We would expect this to hold regardless of the complexity of technology and task environment. These will affect the number and nature of subdivisions within the functional areas, but should not change the functional division of headquarters.

What we have referred to earlier as the long-linked, vertically integrated organization is the prime example. It faces two kinds of continuous problems: (1) the efficient operation of each phase of the total effort, or each function, and (2) coordination of each phase into a master schedule which is responsive to changing environmental conditions. The logical structure to meet continuous problems of this sort is one which divides the organization into units such as purchasing, manufacturing, sales, and transportation; but subordinates each to central planning and scheduling. Grouping in this manner focuses responsibility for efficiency of an activity on those who perform it, and isolates the unit from the action of other variables. Central planning permits the adjustment of each functional activity to the needs of the larger organization through adjustment of the premises on which functional decisions rest. Chandler (1962) found that, in contrast to copper companies, steel enterprises had a greater volume of goods, a larger number of customers, and highly integrated production; all of which combined to require a centralized, functionally departmentalized type of structure to handle the complications in scheduling operations and coordinating functional activities.

This kind of organization may be further subdivided on regional or functional bases, but the number and nature of such subdivisions will vary from organization to organization, as will the amount of discretion exercised at these outposts. Heterogeneity and dynamism of the environment make for the scattering of discretion among many subunits, but this always is relative to the organization's surveillance capacity. Thus Chandler notes that such firms as National Dairy and American Can recentralized when their markets became more nearly homogeneous with urbanization and industrialization of the nation. On the other hand, many firms have recently recentralized as electronic data processing has increased their capacity for surveillance by decreasing the time required to acquire knowledge about environmental fluctuations and plan adjustments.

The organization which we earlier described (Chapter 2) as performing a mediating role and operating extensively also illustrates this proposition. Although from a distance the major divisions of such organizations might appear to be regional, which turns out to be true of the boundary-spanning components, these, in turn, are subordinated to a functional division at the overarching central headquarters. The insurance firm's central office seeks to standardize underwriting so that comparable risks in all regions are covered under common protection and with standard charges, but its headquarters also seeks to schedule the activities of its investment division to fit the flow of revenue inward from policy sales and outward for claim settlements. The merchandising chain's overarching central headquarters usually will be divided functionally along such lines as purchasing, transportation, and sales. Purchasing may then be subdivided functionally into subsections, transportation into regional subsections, and the sales division on regional or functional lines or both. Whatever the internal division of the several functional units, central headquarters performs an essential scheduling activity. Chandler (1962) notes that Sears (one of the most complex of the mediating type of organization) ultimately created a number of semi-autonomous, multifunction divisions, but that Sears' structure differed from that of the complex manufacturers because its central headquarters retained central control over manufacturing and purchasing units.

Proposition 6.4: Under conditions of complexity, when the major components of an organization are reciprocally interdependent, these components will be segmented and arranged in self-sufficient clusters, each cluster having its own domain.

The structure we refer to here is known by several names: in industry it may be called a *product division* or a *profit center,* or it may in general usage be known as a *decentralized division.* During World War II the United States military effort was structured into several theaters of operation, each having a self-contained military capacity.

Our general argument for this proposition is that boundary-spanning components facing heterogeneous and dynamic environments have serious adaptive problems; if they are, in addition, reciprocally interdependent with a technical core which itself is complex, the resulting set of constraints and contingencies exceeds the organization's capacity to adapt and coordinate. By identifying several separable domains and organizing its technical-core and boundary-spanning components in clusters around each domain, the organization attains a realistic bounded rationality.

The diversified organization (Chapter 4) will consist of several conditionally autonomous organizations, each corresponding to one of the domains of the total organization. Thus such a diversified giant as General Electric has vast capacities for marketing, purchasing, and production; but these are not structured into a total marketing division separate from a total purchasing or production division. Rather, each component is segmented and the appropriate segments are assigned to one or another of the profit-center organizations which comprise General Electric.

Chandler (1962) makes it clear, however, that only those industrial organizations making and selling quite different lines of products to increasingly differentiated groups of customers have turned to the new multidivisional form of organization, whereas those that sold a large variety of one major line of products in much higher volume to a greater number of industries and businesses have consistently centralized the control of their activities through developing and rationalizing their functionally departmentalized structures.

We must note that some organizations are structured like the integrated, autonomous division without ever having been part of a larger entity. Voluntary community hospitals and universities, for example, are usually of this type. When the technical and environmental complexity requiring an integrated, autonomous organization arises after an organization has acquired multiple domains, decentralization will appear to be evolutionary; when such complexity arises before the organization has acquired multiple domains, it will remain a single-domain organization.

Chandler sums up the evolution of the integrated, autonomous division in such firms as du Pont, General Motors, Jersey Standard, and Sears: communication and authority channels become clearly inadequate, and responsibility for expanding the firm's share of the market becomes hard to pin down, as demand and taste fluctuate differently in different markets. The separate, integrated division which evolves places on its manager responsibility for the coordination of functional activities to changing demand and taste (p. 393).

To us, the important lesson in Chandler's historical analysis is not that organizations go through a fixed sequence with the integrated, autonomous division as the ultimate structure. Instead, the lesson appears to be that organizations adapt their structures to handle constraints and contingencies.

The decentralized version is, of course, conditionally autonomous, with central headquarters providing some of the premises for decision and, usually, some resources including financial and research. The fully integrated, single-domain organization, such as the community hospital or junior college, may lack such parental protection, but may obtain some of the benefits of large-scale activities by coalescing with similar units and forming "federations" or "associations" (Sills, 1957).

The core of our arguments about structure can now be summarized.

First, organizations face the constraints inherent in their technologies and task environments. Since these differ for various organizations, the basis for structure differs and there is no "one best way" to structure complex organizations.

Second, within these constraints, complex organizations seek to minimize contingencies and to handle necessary contingencies by isolating them for local disposition. Since contingencies arise in different ways for various organizations, there is a variety of structural responses to contingency.

Third, where contingencies are many, organizations seek to cluster capacities into self-sufficient units, each equipped with the full array of resources necessary for the organization to meet contingencies. This means, in effect, that variables controlled by the organization are subordinated to the constraints and contingencies it cannot escape. The more its technology and task environment tend to tear it apart, the more the organization must guard its integrity.

We would expect, therefore, that organizations facing many contingencies would exhibit quite rigorous control over those variables they do control; and this helps explain the paradox that the total institution (operating an intensive technology which penetrates and is penetrated by the environmental object it seeks to change, and therefore so highly vulnerable to many major contingencies) is so highly routinized in many respects. Goffman (1957), in describing total institutions, refers to "batching," which enables the prison or the hospital, for example, to remove variations from many aspects of the organization and thus provide boundaries for rationality where its constraints and contingencies are greatest.

The ever-present conflict between custody and therapy in organizations using the intensive technology revolves around this double requirement for standardization and flexibility. Similar tensions, termed *line and staff conflict*, appear in other types of complex organizations (Dalton, 1959).

In asserting that the three types of interdependence form a Guttman-type scale, we are offering a definition of complexity; but we can restate the relationship between complexity and interdependence in the other direction: the more complex the organization, the more likely its grass-roots groups will be involved in multiple types of interdependence. And to the extent that such a relationship holds, we can also expect the grass-roots groups to be subject to multiple forms of coordination. In the highly complex organization, grass-roots groups are themselves providing some important coordination through mutual adjustment, but their actions are simultaneously circumscribed by schedules and by standardized procedures or rules emanating from elsewhere.

Inevitably, with this much complexity, the coordinating decisions coming from separate sectors and often from separate hierarchical levels will, from time to time, fail to mesh. The result may be dilemmas for those involved, as well as issues for novelists (where the individual usually is forced to choose between safe conformity to rules and programs and a risky attempt to achieve instrumental rationality through violation of rules). The same sort of issue, but analyzed at a higher level, is described as *displacement of goals* through overcommitment to means. Generally this is explained in personality terms as a matter of motivation (Merton, 1957a). Without doubting that some personalities exploit such possibilities, we would like to suggest that these out-of-synchronization episodes are especially prevalent during periods of significant changes in technology or in task environments, and foreshadow the need for *reorganization*, perhaps in the form of regrouping or reclustering, perhaps through decentralization or recentralization.

Although reorganization is a frequent phenomenon in complex organizations in modern societies, our social-scientific understanding of it is meager and largely derived as a by-product. A number of studies of executive succession (Argyris, 1953; Gouldner, 1954; Grusky, 1963; Guest, 1962; Carlson, 1962) bear tangentially on reorganization. We have learned something about reorganization from a number of studies of goal succession (Zald, 1963) and especially in prisons and mental hospitals where therapeutic goals have challenged custodial goals (Cloward, 1960; Grusky, 1959; Rosengren, 1964). Occasionally we also find studies of technological innovations and their impact on structure, such as Janowitz' (1959) analysis of the consequences of new weapons systems on military organization and leadership styles, or studies of the impact of the computer (Shultz and Whisler, 1960). In spite of such research, it seems fair to say that reorganization represents a more pervasive phenomenon than our studies indicate. Yet as the pace of technological change increases and as host environments become more complicated and more dynamic, organizations are having to learn to be more flexible and adaptive. The integrated, autonomous division discussed above is an obvious device for this, although Chandler's analysis (1962) makes clear that this device was anything but obvious to those who developed it through trial and error.

Another device seems gradually to be evolving, another form of organization designed especially for flexibility and adaptability, under such labels as *task force* or *project management.*

Proposition 6.5: Organizations designed to handle unique or custom tasks, and subject to rationality norms, base specialists in homogeneous groups for "housekeeping" purposes, but deploy them into task forces for operational purposes.

The prototype for this kind of organization structure is what Stinchcombe (1959) described as the "craft form of administration," and it is illustrated in the home-construction industry, where a general contractor assembles a task force by drawing individuals from pools of specialized craftsmen. The task-force system is also illustrated by what we have called the synthetic organization, which arises to deal with recovery efforts in community disasters. The principle is more easily seen in those illustrations than within the single organization, but we believe highly complex organizations are groping their way to it.

The modern general hospital, for example, includes specialized groups for housekeeping; for purchasing, billing, etc.; for pharmaceutical supply; for nursing, medicine, and surgery. Some of these groups, such as the business offices and pharmacy, perform their activities as groups. But in those areas where professional knowledge and skills are brought to bear on peculiar, individual cases, the task-force structure is employed. Here the pool of specialists may schedule the availability and deployment of specialists, but may not be involved in supervision of their actual performance. The hospital nurse is thus responsible to a chief nurse who determines her work schedule and place of assignment, but the nurse is responsible to the attending physician in the case of each particular patient.

Traditionally the American university has placed historians in one department, physicists in another, because the faculties and students of either were more interdependent with one another than with those in the other field. But as the American university has taken on new projects —liberal arts curricula, undergraduate specializations or majors, graduate curricula, adult education and public service, and interdisciplinary research efforts—its academic departments have increasingly become pools from which professional talents are allocated. The task-force system emerges most clearly in the university, however, in connection with the education of future faculty members in terminal-degree programs; the doctoral committee appointed to guide and examine the advanced student is a case in point.

Where organizations employ the task-force principle, it appears that coordination through mutual adjustment is accomplished within the task force, that coordination through scheduling is accomplished within the groups from which specialists are dispatched, but that to a considerable extent the rule-making aspect of coordination resides in occupational or professional associations external to the organization. We will have more to say about professional associations and guilds and their impact on organizations in Chapter 9.

RECAPITULATION

Whereas coordination is a central problem for the technical core of the organization, adjustment to constraints and contingencies not controlled by the organization is the crucial problem for boundary-spanning components. Bounded rationality is necessary, and (Prop. 6.1) organizations facing heterogeneous task environments seek to identify homogeneous segments and establish structural units to deal with each. These units (Prop. 6.2) are further subdivided to match surveillance capacity to environmental action, which varies with the degree of stability of the environment faced by the unit in question.

Combining these considerations with those of Chapter 5, we believe that (Prop. 6.3) when technical-core and boundary-spanning activities can be isolated from one another except for scheduling, organizations will be centralized with an overarching layer of functional divisions.

When technical-core and boundary-spanning components are reciprocally interdependent, however (Prop. 6.4), such components will be segmented and arranged in self-sufficient clusters, each cluster having its own domain. This is the major form of decentralization.

Finally (Prop. 6.5), organizations designed to handle unique or custom tasks will base specialists in homogeneous groups for housekeeping purposes, but deploy them into task forces for operational purposes.

These, and the propositions offered in earlier chapters, have consistently referred to norms of rationality, as if rationality were easily measured and standards easily applied. It is time to consider some of the subtleties involved in the assessment of organizational action, and we will do so in Chapter 7.

7

the assessment of organizations

As purposive entities, complex organizations are constantly being evaluated, both by elements of the task environment and by components of the organizations themselves.

Under norms of rationality we might expect organizations to be evaluated in terms of maximum attainment of purposes. The assumption that organizations *maximize,* or seek to, is frequently made about organizations engaged in the private sector of the economy. The maximizing assumption is challenged, however, by those who believe organizations *satisfice,* or seek to attain acceptable or desirable states (Simon, 1957b; March and Simon, 1958; Cyert and March, 1963. See also Baumol, 1959, and Margolis, 1958).

The twin notions of maximizing and satisficing are reflections of the two approaches to complex organizations, rational and natural system, with which we started; and part of the controversy surrounding them stems from these different starting points. The controversy is further confused by the fact that some protagonists refer to *results*, what they believe organizations actually accomplish; while others focus on *motivation*, what they believe organizations try to accomplish.

The controversy over maximizing and satisficing has pulled attention away from what is a more crucial problem, at least from the point of view of the organization, of how organizations *keep score.* Even if we concede that organizations sometimes maximize, the organizational question is whether the organization has any way of knowing that it has done so. And how does it assess itself on the ultimate question, its fitness for the future?

We asserted in Chapter 2 that instrumental or purposive action is rooted on the one hand in desired outcomes and on the other hand in beliefs about cause/effect relationships, and we would also expect these to be the basic variables for the assessment of organization action and readiness for action.

THE VARIABLES OF ASSESSMENT

Assessment inevitably involves some *standard of desirability* against which actual or conceivable effects of causal actions can be evaluated. Assessment also requires determination of what those effects actually are or would be. In the abstract, these two problems in assessment are easily solved; in reality this is another matter. There is nothing automatic about standards of desirability nor is knowledge of effects always easily come by. For organizations in action, these are variables, and our problem now is to conceive of them as such.

Standards of Desirability

Cultures provide general standards of desirability. In our culture, for example, it is considered normal to prefer health over illness, wealth over poverty, life over death, rationality over irrationality, success over failure. Those who would reverse the ratings are considered abnormal. The maximizing notion rests on these tendencies, requiring selection of that unique alternative from among all possible alternatives which unquestionably yields the most on some unidimensional utility scale. Traditionally in the economic model of rationality, the utility is profit, and the assumption is that profit is maximized.

There are no conceptual problems here so long as we are working in a one-dimensional sphere, so long as the question is whether we prefer health over illness or wealth over poverty. But difficulties can arise when we are asked to choose between health and wealth, for this involves a comparison of two dimensions rather than high and low points on a single dimension. In practice the problem becomes even more difficult, for often the choice is not between absolutes but between, for example, some degree of health and some degree of wealth.

People, and organizations, do make choices in multidimensional situations, using some sort of calculus which facilitates preferential ranking of effects regardless of the dimension on which they occur. In classical economic theory the monetary scale plays this role, allowing the economic man to compare all possible effects in terms of a common denominator.

We also know the phenomenon of ambivalence: to eat or to have one's cake. Forced to choose in such a situation, we reveal some preference ranking; but the process of such choice may be a very trying one precisely because it requires construction of a utility scale or the conscious thinking through of beliefs about desirability which had heretofore been latent.

It is not unrealistic, therefore, to conceive of the variable standard of desirability as varying from *crystallized* to *ambiguous*.

Understanding of Cause/Effect Relations

In simple closed systems, knowledge of cause/effect relationships may be complete. Results for every combination of variables can be known from experience or computed because all consequences of action are contained within the system and all causes of action stem from within it. In the complicated open system, however, causal actions often have multiple effects which ramify in different directions and varying distances into the future. Effects within the system may stem from action outside it.

In complexity, then, some consequences of action may be known, some suspected but not proved, and still others unnoticed (Merton, 1936). Realistically, then, we must consider that understanding of cause/effect relationships can vary from complete to incomplete. More importantly for our purposes, the individual or organization engaged in assessment may *believe* that its understanding of cause/effect is *complete* or *incomplete*.

Situations and Types of Assessment

By combining our two dimensions and working only with their extreme values, we have four possible types of assessment situations:

		Complete	Incomplete
		Beliefs about cause/effect knowledge	
	Crystallized	I	II
Standards of desirability	**Ambiguous**	III	IV

What sorts of assessment techniques might we expect in each of these cells?

In Cell I, where cause/effect understanding is believed complete and a standard of desirability is crystallized, we would expect the maximizing approach to assessment. In operational terms this generally is known as the *efficiency test,* and refers to the degree to which perfection is approached. (Strict maximization considers only two classes of outcomes, maximized or nonmaximized; whereas efficiency allows for relativity.) This permits assessment of whether a given effect was produced with least cost or, alternatively, whether a given amount of resources was used in a way to achieve the greatest result.

In Cell II, where a standard of desirability is crystallized but the assessor believes his knowledge of cause/effect is incomplete, the efficiency test is inappropriate, for there is no way of assessing the net effects of causal action. In this case, the appropriate test is not the economic one but the instrumental one—whether a desired state of affairs is achieved (Chapter 2).

The instrumental test is less strict than the one which assesses whether or not a desirable effect is achieved economically. (But the fact that the instrumental test is weaker than the efficiency test does not mean that instrumentalness is unimportant.) In the case of efficiency, what is acceptable or satisfactory or desirable is the maximum; there satisficing and maximizing are identical. In the instrumental case, the assessor is forced to seek another standard of satisfactoriness.

When standards of desirability are ambiguous (Cells III and IV), the assessor must find other means of resolving his dilemma. The literature of complex organizations is not very helpful on this matter, but we can find suggestions in some important work in social psychology.

Studying the stability of individuals' beliefs or opinions, Festinger (1950) noted that group pressures had little influence on those beliefs when the individual had empirical confirmation for them readily at hand, but that group pressures exerted considerable influence on attitudes which lacked such empirical anchorage. This led them to distinguish *empirical* from *social* referents as anchors for opinions or beliefs of individuals.

In somewhat related work, the concept of *reference group* has been useful. Introduced by Hyman (1942) and developed by Merton (1957b) and others, the concept refers to a social category used by the individual as a standard for self-evaluation. The notion was employed, for example, to help explain the wartime finding that soldiers whose chances for rapid promotion were not good were actually better satisfied with promotion chances than were soldiers whose chances were quite good (Stouffer et al., 1949). The evidence indicated that the two categories of soldiers employed quite different reference groups; those with poor chances compared themselves with others who progressed slowly; those with good chances compared themselves with others who progressed rapidly.

Now we want to suggest that when standards of desirability are ambiguous or when cause/effect knowledge is believed incomplete, organizations turn to (social) reference groups. This immediately confronts us with one of the central questions raised by reference-group theory: to which reference groups does the organization turn? We will explore this as we proceed.

Our central problem in the remainder of this chapter will be to speculate about the assessment situations faced by complex organizations and the types of assessments employed. We will start with the following:

Proposition 7.1: Under norms of rationality, assessors prefer efficiency tests over instrumental tests, and instrumental tests over social tests.

Where efficiency tests are valid, they provide a tangibility that is indisputable. Assessment cannot be challenged, and the test is the strictest possible one. With the instrumental test, however, assessment (and hence the assessor) can be uneasy, for there always is the possibility that a better way exists. Where social referents are involved, differences of opinion are possible and, moreover, the referent may be rather unstable.

For the organization as a totality, the important question is not what it has accomplished but its fitness for future action.

Proposition 7.2: At the institutional level (Parsons, 1960, and Chapter 1 above), organizations subject to norms of rationality measure their fitness for the future in satisficing terms.

Organizations face futures which by definition are uncertain. They can never be sure what effects they would like to bring about in this uncertain future.

The organization's fitness is also of concern to task-environment elements (and to elements of the residual environment who might contemplate relations with the organization). Even if the organization itself were convinced of its readiness for the future, its measurements must lead these significant others to the same conclusion. Their judgments, right or wrong, are part of the reality the organization must face. On this question, social reference groups are inescapable.

The image presented by the organization, moreover, is not one image but a variety of images; for the various environmental elements contribute differently to the organization and have different interests to be satisfied through the relationship. We would expect them to be especially interested in the capacity of the organization to satisfy whatever interests they believe will be important in their futures.

Thus, the complex organization is constantly being assessed by a variety of assessors, each inclined to employ a different kind of yardstick; and these are often incompatible. The investor measures the business firm differently than do its dealers or customers, and its employees use still another set of criteria. To score better with one, it may be necessary to divert resources from an area of vital interest to another. The hospital is evaluated on one set of grounds by patients, on another set by medical personnel, and on still a third set by third-party payers such as Blue Cross or welfare agencies. Employers of the university's graduates have a different set of criteria for assessing the university than do its alumni, and the faculty employ still different measures. Prisoners, guards, and legislative groups emphasize different aspects when evaluating the prison.

On the question of fitness of the total organization for future action, then, neither of the prime requirements for efficiency measures (cause/effect certainty and crystallized standards of desirability) is present. Organizations must resort to satisficing measures, but from what sources shall they draw their standards of satisfactoriness?

Proposition 7.2a: Under norms of rationality, organizations facing relatively stable task environments seek to demonstrate fitness for future action by demonstrating historical improvement.

Lacking an absolute or crystallized scale for evaluation, the organization must find a relative one, and the reference group in this case is the organization itself, at an earlier period. In a stable environment, acceptable performance in the past can be taken as evidence of preparedness for the future. Demonstrable improvement over the past lays the basis for the claim of even more satisfactory future performance and hence indicates response to the norm of rationality. Where cause/effect relations are uncertain, improvement in the ratio of successful actions to failures can be taken as evidence of increased rationality.

Because the historical-improvement test is widely used, growth of an organization is often considered a sign of health.

Proposition 7.2b: Under norms of rationality, organizations facing dynamic task environments seek to score favorably in relation to comparable organizations.

Historical improvement may be relevant for all organizations, for environments are never so unstable as to negate the past completely. But in a dynamic task environment there is considerable uncertainty about what the organization may be called upon to achieve in the future, and improvement on obsolete criteria may be of little consequence. Lacking absolute criteria of fitness, and being unable to assume that improvement over its past capability is a reflection of its future, the complex organization then turns to social references to demonstrate that it is doing as well as or better than others in its league.

Business firms in fast-moving industries seek to increase their share of the market, which indicates that in comparison with relevant others, they are fit. They also seek to assure investors, dealers, and employees that their research expenditures compare favorably with those of comparable organizations, that they have more or better product improvements under development, or that new products being designed will more than maintain their present health.

Universities seek to demonstrate that the quality of their student bodies or faculties is increasing more rapidly than the average, or than specific others against which the organizations compete.

But with multiple assessors to be satisfied and scarce resources, the organization may not be able to demonstrate improvement on all criteria. How do organizations solve this ambiguity of standards?

Proposition 7.3: When the organization cannot hope to show improvement on all relevant dimensions, it seeks to hold constant on some and show improvement on those of interest to task-environment elements on which the organization is most dependent.

Recalling our earlier discussion of power and dependence (Chapter 3), we can suggest that when the organization needs a task-environment element more than the element needs the organization, the organization will attempt to score well on dimensions of interest to that element.

Because money, including credit, is a very generalized resource and those who have it can direct it into alternative channels, financial elements of the task environment are usually not highly dependent on a particular organization; and under most circumstances, we would expect organizations to seek to score well on measures of interest to financial supporters. But although financial considerations loom large in the evaluation of most organizations' fitness for the future, the dependence of the organization is never confined to financial sectors of the task environment.

The business firm with capital requirements seeks to demonstrate capacity for future growth and earnings, but at the same time it may seek to convince the powerful union of its ability to benefit employees and to convince potential customers of its ability to provide repairs and services in the future. The public school seeks to convince taxpayers that it can keep expenditures at a minimum consistent with some quality standard, but at the same time it may try to convince parents that it is improving its quality standards. The hospital may try to convince donors and patients that its costs are the least possible, while it assures medical personnel and patients that the quality of care will not be sacrificed to economic criteria.

Proposition 7.4: Under norms of rationality, complex organizations are most alert to and emphasize scoring well on those criteria which are most visible to important task-environment elements.

Business firms whose stocks are traded on public exchanges, for example, are particularly sensitive to the daily quotations of their stock, not because the firm engages in daily stock transactions, but because the market represents a visible social judgment about the firm's fitness for the future. Market changes resulting from publicly known developments, of which the firm is aware, may cause little reaction within the firm. But we would expect considerable anxiety within the firm when the market judgment indicated a change in the firm's future for which the firm itself could not account.[1] Declines for which the organization has no explanation suggest that others have knowledge about the firm or its environment which the firm should have but lacks; unexplained market advances suggest that outsiders see opportunities of which the organization is not aware.

Schools, universities, and hospitals are particularly sensitive to accrediting evaluations, not because these are necessarily believed to reflect or contribute to the quality of the institution or to its intrinsic fitness for the future, but because such evaluations are especially visible. Mental hospitals can likewise emphasize such items as admission and discharge rates, average costs, and similar measures, not because they are measures of the quality of care, but because they are especially visible criteria from which improvement, historically or in comparison with others, can be shown (Jones and Sidebotham, 1962). Public schools are sensitive to measures of pupil hours in various activities, to student-teacher ratios, to drop-out rates, or to dollars spent per pupil per year. None of these is necessarily a reflection of intrinsic achievement or preparation for future intrinsic value, but they are visible criteria from which improvement can be demonstrated (Callahan, 1962). Finding it difficult to judge the quality of faculty research, universities can measure number of publications, research grants received, or jobs offered to faculty. The academic market place (Caplow and McGee, 1958) turns out to be an important mechanism for the evaluation of academic organizations.

Proposition 7.5: When organizations find it difficult to score on intrinsic criteria, they seek extrinsic measures of fitness for the future.

This proposition is broad enough to cover the "red-herring" case where attention is focused on extrinsic measures in order to distract assessors from intrinsic weaknesses. This undoubtedly is a short-run ploy frequently practiced, but we doubt that it is of long-run importance, for it seems unlikely that extrinsic plums will continue to accrue indefinitely to the organization which is failing on available intrinsic criteria. However, there are two more important conditions covered by the above proposition.

Proposition 7.5a: When task-environment elements lack technical ability to assess performance, organizations seek extrinsic measures of fitness for future action.

---

[1] This point was impressed upon me during conversations with my colleague Joseph Pois, of the University of Pittsburgh.

Here we are returning to Perrow's concept of extrinsic prestige (Chapter 3). His hospital study (1961b) brought out the point that such prestige was sought when important elements of the task environment lacked ability to understand and interpret evidences of intrinsic merit. It may be the case, for example, that an organization is engaged in such specialized undertakings with highly refined technologies that few elements of its task environment are capable of evaluating it on technical grounds.

We must recognize, however, that at the institutional level, organizations themselves as well as task-environment elements may lack objective measures of past success or fitness for the future, and that extrinsic measures of quality may be as important for internal purposes as for public relations.

Proposition 7.5b: When cause/effect knowledge is believed incomplete, organizations seek extrinsic measures of fitness for future action.

The norm that authority should be commensurate with responsibility is one reflection of this; when outcomes are beyond the organization's control, assessment in terms of outcomes is resisted (Simon, Guetzkow, Kozmetsky, and Tyndall, 1954) and we would expect this to be especially true when organizations are operating incomplete technologies.

Studying treatment-oriented social work agencies which were forced to use professional services of uncertain validity, such as social casework and group counseling, Eaton found considerable antagonism toward *evaluative research* and a preference for *symbolic research* (Eaton, 1962). In these agencies, daily operations were evaluated on such criteria as number of cases seen, frequency of remission and cures, and testimonials about the value of a practice by clients and their families.

Neither the public school nor the university has proof positive that the student it produces is well educated. The proof is in a lifetime, and the effects of the educational organization can hardly be separated from other influences on that individual. But the fellowships won by its students, and occupational-placement statistics can be compiled quickly. The classroom performance of professors is difficult to judge, but the university can point to honors won by its faculty as evidence of its quality.

The use of extrinsic measures of fitness for the future has the special advantage that they can be employed selectively. For alumni, donors, parents, students, and even fellow faculty members, success on extrinsic measures can be presented without evidence of lack of success. Thus honors won can be tabulated for a faculty without computing or revealing percentages of honors won to honors sought. (See any alumni magazine.)

ORGANIZATIONAL ASSESSMENTS OF COMPONENTS

Whatever their outward images, complex organizations seek to evaluate intrinsically the fitness of their components for future action; and because efficiency measures are the strictest and most precise, we would expect them to employ efficiency measures where possible.

Proposition 7.6: When technologies are instrumentally perfected, and task environments stable or well buffered, organizations under rationality norms measure components in terms of (past) efficiency.

The instrumentally perfected technology affords complete understanding of cause/effect relationships, including all reasonable alternatives, and permits identification of the separate contributions of interdependent units. Environmental stability offers assurance that the technology previously used will be relevant in the future. Under these conditions, efficiency of past action is indicative of readiness to act rationally in the future.

We would expect this situation to be approximated in highly automated mass production technologies, and perhaps most closely achieved in continuous-process chemical activities such as petroleum refineries. Although perhaps with slightly less perfection, we would generally expect efficiency measures to be dominant in core technologies of the long-linked variety where repetition of the technology provides experience for relative certainty about cause and effect, and where buffering mitigates the effects of exogenous variables. For a given size of output and known constraints, it is possible to compute the minimum amounts of resources that would be expended if the unit were efficient (or given a certain amount of resource inputs, to calculate the amount of output that could possibly result). Any deviation from these standards is considered an indication of failure to maximize. Thus, under relatively stable conditions, cost, quantity, and quality become the key assessment variables in core technologies of mass production organizations.

Proposition 7.7: Where task environments are relatively stable or well buffered and knowledge of cause and effect believed reasonably complete, organizations under rationality norms seek to account for interdependence and to assess each unit in efficiency terms.

Efficiency measurements are valid only if effects can be attributed to the appropriate causal action and only if the effects of causal action can be traced. Under these conditions *suboptimization* is possible and appropriate, meaning that the outcomes of a particular unit are maximized within constraints established for the benefit of other units and ultimately the entire organization. Here management science or operations research has important applications, but where knowledge of cause/effect relations is incomplete, efficiency can be computed only if costs and contributions are arbitrarily assigned.

To the extent that statistical or quantitative accounting devices can be established to isolate the effects of each unit in an interdependent constellation of units, or to assign consequences to particular time periods, organizations can measure efficiency or optimality against known standards. Under rationality norms, the tendency to quantify for precision measurement is probably the major reason for the emergence of cost-accounting techniques in all types of complex organizations where actions are measured in monetary units, and for the proliferation of statistical techniques where units of measure are other than monetary.

Such arbitrary procedures for attributing costs and contributions by interdependent units are found not only in the business firm but also, for example, in hospital pharmacies or dietary departments, in schools in connection with purchasing of supplies and operation of bus systems, and in universities where costs of instruction are apportioned among teaching departments. The most dramatic example, however, remains in those business firms which rely on *transfer pricing* to compute the contributions of various interdependent units as if they were independent. Transfer pricing is often found in firms of the horizontally integrated variety, where two or more divisions are sequentially interdependent. The earlier division "sells" its product to the later division, which "buys" its input from within the organization. Transfer pricing is an attempt to substitute arbitrarily for the missing market mechanism or external measuring group, whose absence is due to the design of the organization. Each unit involved is expected to behave as if it were independent with respect to the other.

Such accounting and statistical devices are also used when time periods as well as component units are interdependent.

The fact that such accounting and statistical schemes are socially invented and validated means that they are more vulnerable to attack than are empirical referents, and leads to some important consequences for the behavior of individuals and groups within organizations. We will give further consideration to this aspect later.

Proposition 7.8: When knowledge of cause/effect relationships is known to be incomplete, organizations under rationality norms evaluate component units in terms of organizational (rather than technical) rationality (Chapter 2).

With clearly imperfect technologies, technical rationality cannot be assessed with confidence, and the organization must fall back to a less precise but fundamental question: does the unit contribute to the organization's needs? The closed system of logic is inapplicable when the technology is imperfect; for, by definition, unrecognized variables are affecting technical results, or known variables are operating in unpredictable ways. The organization must therefore rely on open-system logics and less precise evidence of fitness for future action.

Proposition 7.8a: Where interdependence is controlled through rules, such units are measured in terms of adherence to or deviation from rules.

Proposition 7.8b: Where interdependence is controlled through scheduling, such units are measured in terms of quota filling.

In both of these propositions, we are saying that efficiency gives way to assessment on the basis of the unit's ability to meet expectations of other units with which it is interdependent. Unable to evaluate in terms of absolute, empirical standards, the organization turns to reference groups; and in this case, the relevant reference groups are the other units which rely on the unit being assessed. In both cases, the measurements may be expressed in quantitative terms—the number of errors in relation to the number of satisfactory actions, or the results of action compared with quotas previously established. But when interdependence is even greater, quantitative evaluation gives way to something less tangible.

Proposition 7.8c: Where interdependence is controlled through mutual adjustment, units are measured in terms of the confidence expressed in them by coordinate units.

Evaluations of this sort are typically made of maintenance or troubleshooting crews; nursing services; instructional teams in schools and universities; advertising, legal, and labor relations departments in business firms; and public relations departments of virtually all types of organizations which contain them. Boundary-spanning units, engaged in direct interdependence with elements of the task environment, are judged in part by evidence of disappointments they cause for elements of the task environments. Boundary-spanning units are always interdependent with other units of the organization and hence are evaluated on technical or organizational rationality, as suggested above. But elements of the task environment always have data about the capacity or performance of these units which are not directly available to the organization itself. This is true, for example, of sales units for the business firm; interviewers for the employment agency (Blau, 1955); tellers for the bank (Argyris, 1954); classroom instructors for the school or university; caseworkers for the welfare agency (Thomas, 1959); or purchasing agents (Strauss, 1962).

In each of these cases, the nonmember is in a position to have information about the performance of a boundary-spanning unit that is not directly available to the organization itself, and we would expect organizations to seek evidence from task-environment elements to supplement internal assessments.

Proposition 7.9: When units operating imperfect technologies are conditionally autonomous, they are measured by extrinsic standards.

Now we are arguing that conditional autonomy removes the unit from scrutiny by associates, and imperfections in the technology prevent evaluation by measuring conformity to standards. Lacking either empirical or social means of evaluating intrinsic merit, the organization turns to still more indirect evidence.

Under these conditions, public relations or advertising departments may be judged within the organization by the recognition they receive from experts outside it, such as public relations or advertising associations. University faculties may be judged within the university by the recognition given their research and publications by others in the relevant professional associations, especially as this is reflected in the academic market. The practice of matching job offers from outside attests to the inability of the university itself to determine the value of its faculty. White's (1961) study of an industrial research and development department indicated that the life of the unit rested not on demonstrated output but on a climate of opinion favorable to research and development in the task environment with which other managers in the firm had the closest connections.

Because units in complex organizations are frequently interdependent with several others, they may be subject to assessment on multiple criteria.

Proposition 7.10: As the organization's posture with respect to the task environment fluctuates, the organization adjusts relative weightings of the multiple criteria by which it evaluates component units.

Dynamic task environments result in shifting power and dependence relations between the organization and its task environment; and as dependency shifts, we can expect it to become more sensitive to evaluations by some elements of the task environment (Prop. 7.3), and less sensitive to others. The university suddenly faced with budgetary problems may reduce its weighting on faculty research and increase its evaluation of faculty performance in bringing new research funds to the organization. The business firm whose reputation for product quality is slipping may shift its evaluating emphasis from quantity or cost to quality, and the manufacturing or construction organization may put a premium on evidence of safety following an accident (Cyert, Dill and March, 1958).

The multiplicity of assessment criteria, together with variability in the weightings accorded each criterion, makes extremely difficult the assessment of organization units in rational-model terms; but as Frank (1958) has shown, it adds considerably to the organization's flexibility in a dynamic environment by forcing members of units to search for clues about shifting weightings.

RECAPITULATION

Under norms of rationality, organizations and others assessing them (Prop. 7.1) prefer efficiency tests over instrumental tests, and instrumental tests over social tests. But efficiency tests are not possible when technical knowledge is incomplete or standards of desirability are ambiguous. Since both of these conditions exist at the institutional level of the organization (Prop. 7.2), fitness for the future is measured in satisficing terms, especially by comparison with past performance or with other organizations.

Organizations are multidimensional, and when they cannot show improvement on all dimensions (Prop. 7.3), they seek to show improvement on those of interest to important elements of the task environment. Organizations (Prop. 7.4) especially emphasize scoring well on criteria which are most visible to important elements of the task environment; and when it is difficult to score on intrinsic criteria (Prop. 7.5), organizations seek extrinsic measures of fitness for the future.

Organizations assess their own components in terms of past efficiency (Prop. 7.6) when technologies are perfected and task environments stable or well buffered. If those conditions are met only reasonably well (Prop. 7.7), organizations seek to account for interdependence and assess each unit in efficiency terms. But where cause/effect knowledge is incomplete (Prop. 7.8), organizations measure components in terms of organizational rationality; or when the unit is too autonomous to be evaluated by other components (Prop. 7.9), extrinsic measures are used. Finally (Prop. 7.10), when units are subject to multiple criteria, organizations adjust their relative weightings as the organization's relations to its task environment fluctuate.

part two

We have offered a number of propositions about what organizations do or what they seek to do. But of course they do nothing except as individual members within them act. We must therefore consider behavior of people in and around organizations if we are to understand the behavior of organizations.

There are several important questions to be dealt with in this connection. One is the extent to which organizations gain a measure of certainty or predictability with respect to the behavior of their members, or of others in the task environment. This is of considerable importance if we stick to our central theme that organizations abhor uncertainty while subject to norms of rationality. If their individual members behave in unpredictable ways, organizations are in difficulty. We will consider these questions in Chapters 8 and 9.

An equally important question concerns the exercise of discretion by organization members, for this is the heart of the administrative process as we see it. In Part One, we have argued at length that organizations are not free agents. But it must also be clear that such factors as technology and task environment seldom completely determine how organizations act. When the immutable facts of organizational life have been faced and the contingencies spelled out, organizations have choices. It is at these points that discretion makes the difference; therefore we must examine the exercise of discretion by human actors in and around organizations.

We will argue that the ability or opportunity to exercise discretion is not uniformly distributed throughout the organization—that technology, task environment, design, and structure result in patterns of discretion. We first need to explore (1) who participates in the exercise of discretion, (2) relationships among such participants, (3) what discretion is about, and (4) how it is expressed. In short, we need to explore the administrative process in terms of our earlier analysis.

8

the variable human

The human actor is a multidimensional phenomenon subject to the influences of a great many variables. The range of differences in aptitude is great, and the learned behavior patterns (considering mankind as a whole) is quite diverse. Neither we nor organizations have the data or the calculus to understand organization members in their full complexity, and the requirements of complicated technologies in complicated task environments cannot be met if the full range of human variations comes into play within the organization.

Components of Purposive Action

Our ability to understand or "account for" human action is governed largely by our choice of accounting scheme or conceptual framework. For the level of understanding we seek here, we shall use a simple scheme patterned after formulations of Lewin (1935), Parsons (1937), and Parsons and Shils (1951), and recent research in cognition and perception.

Our basic formulation is that human action emerges from the interaction of (1) the individual, who brings *aspirations, standards,* and *knowledge or beliefs about causation;* and (2) the situation, which presents *opportunities* and *constraints.* Interaction of the individual and the situation is mediated by his perceptions or cognitions.

Thus we assume that the purposive individual will try to exploit his opportunities (as he sees them) in the direction of his aspirations and that, within the limits of the constraints he believes to be operating, he will be guided in this endeavor by his beliefs about causation and by the standards or norms he believes are appropriate.

A major advantage of this accounting scheme is that it allows us to search in two directions, in the individual and in his environment, for sources of diversity and uniformity. To the extent that individuals bring similar aspirations, beliefs, and standards into situations appearing to offer similar opportunities and constraints, we can expect to find similarities or patterns in the ensuing action. We now need to explore the extent to which categories of individuals are similarly programmed, and situations in complex organizations are similarly structured.

UNIFORMITIES AMONG INDIVIDUALS

Homogenizing Influences of Culture

Of the many knowable ways of behaving in specific kinds of situations, the individual knows only a few. Of the several hundred known languages, most individuals know only a handful at best. The repertoire of behavior patterns is confined primarily to those having currency in their culture, and one of the significant aspects of culture for any society is that it frees individuals from having to make deliberate choices from among hosts of possibilities. This is true not only with regard to such basic items as which foods are edible, which language shall be the native one, or appropriate forms of religious observance; but it applies equally well to matters more obviously related to organizations—ways of perceiving and categorizing reality (Lee, 1950); beliefs about cause/effect relationships, definitions of legitimacy, and attitudes toward authority (Miller, 1955); orientations toward time (Hall, 1959); and personal aspirations (McClelland, 1961). Definitions of the worthwhile life and methods of assessing success are highly determined by the culture, which thus limits the range of aspirations current in a society.

The homogenizing influences of culture are most clearly seen in societies in transition to modernization, where the contrasts between those factors which are conducive to complex organizations and the inherited aspirations and beliefs, the perceptions and interpretations of reality, are sharp and the entrenched homogeneity thus highly visible (Moore and Feldman, 1960; Harbison and Myers, 1959). Indeed, the norms of rationality which accompany complex organizations may be at odds with the basic values and orientations of such cultures. The cultures of transitional societies, moreover, typically do not incorporate the skills required for the operation of complicated technologies (Stinchcombe, 1965).

In the transitional society, then, the homogenizing influences of culture appear as constraints on organizations, as factors retarding organization action under rationality norms. These constraints are real indeed, but the fact that potential members have in common standardized ways of viewing the world and of communicating, means that the organization is spared the impossible task of dealing with *random* discrepancies between what it needs and what exists.

In societies geared to complex organizations—sometimes referred to as *industrialized societies,* but also geared to the operation of complex organizations for governmental, military, educational, medical, and other purposes—the homogenizing effect of culture is often unnoticed. The society geared to complex organizations is a diverse one, containing variations in knowledge and skills, aspirations, beliefs about causation, and many other things. This society becomes, for practical purposes, a multicultured society, but its cultures remain subordinate to some common themes. Complex organizations in such societies can and do take for granted that virtually all members will share a common language, common conceptions of time, a common arithmetic system, and a host of similar patterns.

It is precisely because these can be assumed that our attention is directed away from the homogeneous aspects and focused on diversity. Yet when we compare complex organizations in one modern society with organizations doing basically similar things in another, the homogenizing influences appear unmistakable. Similarities of core technologies notwithstanding, complex organizations in Germany bear the stamp of German culture (Harbison et al., 1955; Hartmann, 1959); those in Britain, the stamp of British culture (Richardson, 1956); and those in Japan, the stamp of Japanese culture (Abbeglan, 1958).

Culture can act as a constraint in the society geared to complex organization as well as in the transitional society, for new technologies can call for talents which only gradually become incorporated into the culture. Generally speaking, however, the problem is one of matching diversity with diverse needs, and we therefore need to examine the operation of the social system.

Channeling Functions of the Social System

Social systems are always structured, and in the society geared to complex organizations, economic activities are clustered into *occupations*. Individuals are sorted and prepared for them and are taught to fashion *careers*, either within an occupation or in some combination of them. Typically the individual does not select from among all occupations contained in his society, nor does he consider all possible careers. Rather through such socialization agencies as the family, the neighborhood, and the school, the young member of the modern society is taught that a limited array of occupations offer meaningful possibilities for him; he is equipped with knowledge of points of entry into those occupations and he is led to understand what constitutes reasonable success in them.

[Much of the difficulty of incorporating complex organizations into transitional societies lies in the absence of this "infrastructure"—the notion of career, aspirations defined in career terms, and the preparatory socializing agencies (Riggs, 1964; Parsons, 1960; Stinchcombe, 1965).]

The sorting and socializing processes which result in an individual's entry into an occupation also holds out to him a limited array of *career prototypes*. Occupations are characterized by a series of more or less well-defined ranks, and the entering individuals know or soon learn whether the experience, skill, or knowledge acquired at a particular level is useful in advancing to the next or in moving into a different occupation. Career prototypes also indicate branching points. The beginner in factory assembly line operations knows or soon learns that there are few ranks through which he can move in that occupation, and if he is to progress beyond it he must leave the occupation for another, usually supervision or self-employment. The nurse knows that nursing ranks are few and that whatever her competence and performance as a nurse, she cannot be promoted to physician; but she also knows that leaving nursing for supervisory work is a reasonable avenue for career building.

Thus depending on his initial position in the social system and his exposure to socializing agencies, the individual typically acquires awareness of and preparation for a small range of occupations. With these he learns one or a few career prototypes which set limits and give direction to his aspirations and provide him with a set of expectations regarding the kind of career it is possible for him to build. Entry into an occupation also provides him with beliefs about cause/effect linkage in building such a career and with standards by which to judge his progress and achievements. Typically, these components of action are synchronized.

Clearly the patterns we are talking about at this point are imperfect, not inevitable. For example, some individuals acquire aspirations for which their knowledge is inadequate. Some find it possible to move from one occupation into a totally unrelated one. Some find, with changing technologies, that career prototypes which pointed to future opportunities were in error. The content of those components of action are also obviously not unchanging for the individual, for he may acquire new aspirations, beliefs, and standards as life unfolds.

Nor are we maintaining that the homogenizing influence of culture and the sorting and channeling functions of the social system eliminate heterogeneity. There remain even within an occupational category differences of temperament, personality, and dexterity; differences in age, experience, and seniority; differences in family circumstances, economic needs, and levels of aspiration.

The fact remains, however, that if the modern society is to be viable it must sort individuals into occupational categories; equip them with relevant aspirations, beliefs, and standards; and channel them to relevant sectors of "the" labor market. On those dimensions most relevant to jobs as defined technologically, each occupational category is relatively homogeneous, and it is this relevant uniformity which enables individuals and organizations to meet in the labor market.

INDUCEMENTS/CONTRIBUTIONS CONTRACTS[1]

The inducements/contributions theory of Barnard (1938), Simon (1957), and March and Simon (1958) asserts that the individual's decision to participate in an organization and the organization's decision to include him rest on a bargained contract—sometimes expressed in great detail, sometimes largely implied or understood—about what each will contribute to the other and each will receive.

The inducements/contributions contract sets limits to the behavior that the individual is to exhibit in the organizational context, thereby further reducing the expression of heterogeneity of humans (Gouldner,

[1] The remainder of this chapter is based largely on ideas generated by Robert W. Avery and Richard O. Carlson and set forth by the three of us in an unpublished paper entitled "Occupations, Personnel and Careers."

1957; Weber, 1947). The contract, explicitly or by implication, also provides limits on the organization; it can call on a limited array of the individual's total repertoire of possible behavior. There remains, however, a "zone of indifference" (Barnard, 1938), or "zone of acceptance" (Simon, 1957), which indicates that within the confines of the contract, the organization may specify any of several modes of behavior and the individual member is indifferent as to which. This zone of indifference provides an area of discretion for the organization, enabling it to define appropriate behavior and to modify that definition from time to time to meet the changing dictates of technology and task environment. In effect, it makes individual members of the organization, despite individual differences, somewhat pliable in the direction of the organization's needs.

Clearly there is a *quid pro quo* theme to the inducements/contributions contract, for it defines what is expected of individuals in terms of jobs needing to be done, and it defines the rewards which the organization pledges for the appropriate performance of such jobs. But if the contract provides the organization with opportunities and constraints with respect to the operation of technologies, it also provides opportunities and constraints for the career-building individual. The job is more than a means of exchanging today's efforts for today's inducements; it has long-term as well as short-term implications.

As a unit in his career, the job provides the individual with an arena or *sphere of action* in which to seek solutions to his career problems, and thus to meet the demands placed on him by the social system. Whatever value he places on occupational-career achievement relative to other dimensions of his life, these other dimensions can seldom be satisfied without some satisfactory solution to the occupational-career problem.

In the society geared to complex organizations, individuals are motivated to protect or enhance their spheres of occupational action (Costello et al., 1963), and this motivation is reflected in the negotiation of inducements/contributions contracts with complex organizations.

Proposition 8.1: In modern societies, the content of the inducements/contributions contract is determined through power (political) processes.

Because the job has different significance for the organization and for the individual, its definition must be the result of consensus, and the contract in existence at any point in time rests on the power of the parties relative to one another. Again we are using Emerson's (1962) concept of power (Chapter 3), which asserts that power is based on the dependence of each party on the other. To the extent that the individual needs access to jobs the organization can provide and lacks other avenues to such jobs, the organization is powerful in the negotiation process. Conversely, to the extent that the organization needs qualified members and cannot get them elsewhere, individuals are powerful in the negotiation process. The ultimate degree of this relationship would be bilateral monopoly (Siegel and Foraker, 1960).

Now we want to explore the possibility that different types of jobs present different power situations and hence call for differences in political action. To do so, we need to be able to distinguish among jobs on dimensions relevant to power and dependence.

One significant dimension on which jobs, considered as action spheres, can vary is the *opportunity to learn* skills, data, and attitudes which are appropriate for other, better jobs. The "assistant-to" position (Whisler, 1960), for example, or the management trouble-shooting job (Dill et al., 1962) affords the individual opportunities to interact with others in more advanced positions and to observe the requirements and behavior patterns for a variety of managerial positions. They provide considerable opportunity to learn from the successful and unsuccessful performances of others. Not all jobs provide such opportunities or provide them in such degree.

A second important dimension on which jobs can vary is the *opportunity for visibility* (Dalton, 1959; Dill et al., 1962; Becker and Strauss, 1956). Jobs in which the individual interacts principally with nonhuman components of the technology, and does so in standardized, repetitive ways, provide little opportunity for favorable visibility. Only if he "goofs" is he likely to be noticed. Other jobs have a much larger human interaction context, and if these also permit or require the occupant to exercise discretion, performance may be noticeable to others. For some jobs these others are seldom members of the organization (Blau, 1964; Argyris, 1954), whereas for some the job interaction is largely or entirely with others in the organization (Howton, 1963).

The interaction context of the job thus delimits or shapes the opportunities of the individual to learn the contents and requirements of other, better jobs, and also his opportunities to be noticed as more than adequate in his present job. While these opportunities are often correlated, it seems possible for some jobs to provide one without the other.

Finally, the *types of assessments* levied by significant others on the individual's performance is an important dimension of variation. This depends on the location of the job in the scheme of technical or organizational rationality, and the resulting feasibility of applying efficiency or satisficing measures to the job and to the individual's performance of it (Chapter 7).

TECHNOLOGIES AND NEGOTIATION STRATEGIES

In terms of the above dimensions, *the action spheres presented by jobs* differ according to the technologies in which those jobs are imbedded.

Action in Routinized Jobs

Jobs in long-linked technologies and in the protected portions of mediating technologies are highly standardized and repetitive, in part because such technologies can operate only when instrumental knowledge is highly developed (Chapter 2), in part because such technologies are removed from environmental contingencies, and in part because organizational structure relates these jobs in relatively fixed patterns (Chapter 5). Such jobs thus tend to be fully determined to the point where discretion, if exercised, is an unwelcome influence that can only result in reduction of efficiency or instrumental rationality. In the society geared to organizations, such jobs are considered "semiskilled" because they are entered with skills widely distributed in the population as part of the general socializing process, or can quickly be developed on the basis of those common skills. (In the transitional society, the same types of jobs may appear to be highly skilled because the necessary abilities are less commonly developed.)

The highly determined nature of such jobs provides little opportunity to learn skills and attitudes appropriate for other jobs, for time and interaction patterns are highly circumscribed. Because the need for discretion has been eliminated from such jobs, visibility of a positive sort is nil; nearly complete knowledge of cause/effect relationships enables the organization to calculate standards of maximum behavior, and any discrepancy between actual and calculated behavior is interpreted in negative terms. Finally, since such jobs are protected from the environment and employ skills commonly available, individuals in the occupation are considered interchangeable and the individual has little opportunity to become visible outside the organization.

The occupations which such jobs represent also typically hold out meager career prototypes. Gradations between entry level and top jobs in the occupation are few, and the climb to that ceiling often comes before the "prime of life"; i.e., before the individual's social needs for economic achievement have been satisfied. [Although "need for achievement" is a psychological concept (McClelland, 1953) it is governed to a large extent by factors in the social system. In the society geared to organizations, for example, entry into the labor market and formation of families typically occur within a short span of years, while economic and status needs continue to climb until the offspring are in turn self-supporting.]

This social context generates strong pressures on individuals in *early-ceiling occupations* to break out of those occupations into new ones with higher and later ceilings. The hope of becoming self-employed, the dream of being selected from the ranks for promotion to a better occupation, or part-time study in preparation for a new occupation are not isolated phenomena. But if the resources needed for self-employment are scarce, visibility for promotion is lacking, or talent for further education is undeveloped—in short, if breaking out of the early-ceiling occupation is inhibited—the last hope for bringing achievements into line with needs is through efforts to protect and enhance the occupation itself (as distinct from enhancing the individual's status within it). Under these conditions, collective action becomes the characteristic strategy for career building.

Proposition 8.2: Inducements/contributions contracts for jobs in routinized technologies are determined through collective bargaining.

We are arguing now that within the boundaries of jobs as determined by routinized technologies, action spheres are indeed meager; and to gain enriched possibilities for building careers, jobholders resort to political (power) processes. They seek to operate on the boundaries of the jobs. Collective action in such technologies is not simply a device for gaining increased *quid pro quo*. It is that, but it is also a device for protecting or enlarging action spheres which are intrinsically meager. Thus in view of the fact that required skills are commonly available and individuals are considered interchangeable, the contract typically includes provisions about job security or job rights. And because the top of the occupation is reached so quickly by so many, visibility based on performance is thwarted, and the contract typically includes provisions for seniority rights. Finally, because technical knowledge is so complete that efficiency standards are employed (Prop. 7.8), the contract typically includes limitations on assessment standards and on their interpretation and application.

(We must recognize the possibility that ideological convictions may lead white-collar workers in routinized technologies to consider unions as appropriate only for blue-collar jobs, as has been traditional in the United States. Such ideological convictions may slow the development of collective bargaining, but the growth of white-collar unions indicates that the pressures for collective action are strong when individuals in meager action spheres are motivated to protect or enhance career opportunities.)

Both parties have strong investments on which the collective bargaining process impinges—organizations in the operation of technologies, and individuals in the building of careers. A change in the relative power of one party with respect to the other can have important consequences for both; hence changes in the rules governing collective bargaining processes can be crucial.

Proposition 8.2a: In collective bargaining, both parties have strong interests in governmental processes which establish the boundaries and rules for collective bargaining.

The ability of collective bargaining agencies to obtain favorable agreements on these issues, however, depends on their ability to deny to the organization access to suitable employees on other terms. Thus the strike becomes a major weapon in negotiations for routinized jobs, and employment of strikebreakers, a major counterweapon. The collective bargaining situation also encourages both parties to seek allies—unions, in the form of confederation with other unions; and employing organizations, in the form of alliances with other employing organizations.

Not only is unionization a characteristic feature of societies geared to complex organizations, it is also a governmental issue in such societies. Hence the forces which give rise to complex organizations for routinized activities also propel such organizations into deeper ties with the larger environment—that is, into wider task environments—than either technology or market forces would imply.

Action in Jobs at Contingent Boundaries

Boundary-spanning jobs vary considerably in the types of action spheres they afford, depending on the degree to which the environment at the boundary is homogeneous or heterogeneous, stable or shifting (Chapter 6). To the extent that the environmental sector is homogeneous and stable, boundary-spanning jobs can be standardized, use common skills, and afford little opportunity for learning or for career-building visibility. Under these conditions, the jobs are routinized, and we would expect the contracts to be negotiated by collective bargaining as discussed above.

To the extent that boundary-spanning jobs occur at points where the task environment is heterogeneous and shifting, however, such jobs require the exercise of discretion to meet contingencies, thus affording opportunities to learn through experience and opportunities for visibility. Assessment standards at these high-contingency boundaries are frequently in terms of organizational rationality (Prop. 7.8) rather than efficiency, and the *quid pro quo* aspect of the inducements/contributions contract may explicitly recognize this element of discretion by hinging remuneration to results, as in "commission" forms of payment.

Whether remuneration is a stated amount or a sliding scale based on results, career ceilings in occupations located at high-contingency boundaries tend to come late. The employee who scores well on a small boundary can expect to be visible, internally or externally or both, and thus have the possibility of bargaining for a job at a larger or more critical sector of the organization or of another organization. Because such jobs can frequently be entered with common skills, but provide late ceilings for individuals able and motivated to exploit them, such boundary-spanning occupations are important avenues for upward social mobility in societies geared to complex organizations.

Proposition 8.3: Inducements/contributions contracts at contingent boundaries of the organization are determined by (*a*) the power of a task-environment element and (*b*) the individual's ability to handle the organization's dependence on that element.

Here again power is the crux of the bargaining process, but in this case individual rather than collective action is characteristic. By permitting individuals to exercise discretion, jobs at contingent boundaries enable individuals to reduce uncertainties for the organization. To the extent that he can contain contingencies and to the extent that the contingencies are important to the organization, the individual is powerful in the bargaining process. Procurement officers are relatively powerful when needed inputs are scarce, less powerful when such inputs are plentiful. Those able to procure large contracts in dynamic task environments are more powerful than those procuring routine supplies in orderly task environments. On the output side of the organization, to the extent that a clientele is problematic for the organization, the individual able to solve that problem has power in the inducements/contributions negotiation. Here career building calls for an orientation to the clientele rather than to the organization; indeed, the individual in such a job often can develop rapport with a clientele group to the point where he can move from one organization to another and take his clients with him.

To the extent that the organization has handled environmental contingencies through structure, it has removed need for discretion from the boundary-spanning job and thus has reduced its dependence on the individual in that job. Thus the organization which has established differentiated units to deal with homogeneous segments of a heterogeneous environment (Prop. 6.1) has removed much of the potential discretion from the boundary-spanning job. Similarly, the organization which has learned the range of environmental variation and has established sets of rules (Prop. 6.2b) has reduced the need for discretion to that of classifying cases.

But structure is not the only device that organizations employ to reduce their dependence on individuals in boundary-spanning jobs; organizations can work to reduce the freedom of task-environment elements.

Proposition 8.3a: To the extent that the organization gains power over task-environment elements, it reduces its dependence on the boundary-spanning jobs which deal with those elements.

Organizational action which reduces the ability of a task-environment element to satisfy its goal elsewhere, increases the power of the organization with respect to that element. The acquisition of prestige (Prop. 3.2) or, more generally, *product differentiation* of an extrinsic nature is one means. Differentiation in intrinsic performance is another, and achievement of monopoly is the extreme form. Where elements of the task environment have no feasible alternative, however, the organization may become dependent on its boundary-spanning members to detect evasive action by those elements (Blau, 1955; Thompson, 1962).

Action in Intensive Technologies

In intensive technologies, where entry into an occupation is usually through specialized training, the inducements/contributions bargain takes on still another set of characteristics. Typically the agencies which provide the necessary training are effective not only at establishing minimum standards but also at controlling entry into training and thereby the supply of those so trained. Thus in the craft occupations the number of apprenticeships is carefully controlled by the guild or union, and in the professions the supply is regulated by guarding the number of approved or accredited training institutions.

Because such occupations rest on specialized skills, there is basis for contention that assessment standards should be established and performance evaluated by peers in the occupation, or by those in higher occupations in the same occupational family, i.e., nurses by doctors, technicians by scientists or engineers. Guilds, craft unions, and professional associations seek to assure that the determination of standards be kept out of lay hands and that organizations employing members of the occupation assess only the results, not the methods, of performance.

Occupations requiring specialized skills usually also require the exercise of discretion and therefore provide opportunities to learn and to gain visibility. The nature of these opportunities, however, depends on whether the occupation has an early or late ceiling. The early-ceiling variety of skilled occupation provides opportunity to learn through experience in exercising discretion and, often, through interaction with members of higher occupations as members of work teams (i.e., the nurse-physician team). But because gradations in early-ceiling occupations are few and the categories standardized, a reputation for reliability, good judgment, and performance beyond the minimum does not travel very far. This visibility, moreover, does not gain entry for the individual into higher occupations in the same family, since the only recognized entry into them is through formal training. Visibility, then, may be used to bargain for preferred assignments and, on occasion, to move out of the occupation into managerial jobs.

Proposition 8.4: Individuals in early-ceiling occupations in intensive technologies seek leverage in the negotiation process through collective action to upgrade the occupation relative to others.

Whether through craft unions or professional associations, these occupations are frequently involved in political action to establish exclusive jurisdictions or delimit jurisdictions. Thus teachers associations may campaign to eliminate from teaching jobs such nonprofessional duties as record keeping and supervision of lunch periods. Nurses associations may campaign to eliminate such nonprofessional activities as housekeeping, and also to expand the professional role into areas previously reserved for physicians. Organizations employing intensive technologies are not infrequently caught up in such jurisdictional disputes between two or more elements of their task environment.

Proposition 8.5: Where the intensive technology employs late-ceiling occupations (professions), the inducements/contributions bargain rests on the individual's visibility among occupational colleagues.

The intensive technology puts a premium on the exercise of discretion and therefore affords opportunities to learn through experience. Visibility within the organization and, frequently, visibility to the lay clientele tend to be high in professional occupations. But unless the profession is a central one for the organization, performance on the job is more visible to laymen than to peers most competent to evaluate merit and reward achievement.

The career problem for the professional usually centers around his ability to increase his skills and to make that increase visible to his colleagues. Since local markets tend to be limited for these occupations, individuals must remain visible to colleagues in national or regional networks through publication in professional journals, participation in seminars, and activities in the professional associations.

To the extent that he maintains such visibility and remains willing to change organizations, the individual's dependence on the organization is reduced and hence its relative power is increased. The inducements/negotiations bargain thus tends to focus on varied experiences which provide enlarged opportunities to learn and freedom to publish and remain active in professional activities.

Action in the Managerial Technology

We have noted that one of the high-ceiling occupations to which those in lower-ceiling occupations can sometimes aspire is supervision, management, or administration—occupations in what we will call the managerial technology. Another way of entering these occupations is through general education at a higher level than that attained through widely dispersed socializing agencies. In the society geared to complex organizations, this may mean that a college education is preparatory for managerial occupations.

The variety of access into these occupations reflects the fact that these occupations call for skills, knowledge, or aptitudes stated only in general terms and measured imprecisely if at all (Goldner, 1965). Hence the specific content of that preparation, educational or prior experience in another occupation, is less significant than evidence that the individual holds values and loyalties deemed important by the organization. Skill requirements are not highly standardized, nor is performance easily measured. There are, therefore, no uniform classifications which are widely recognized. Once launched in the occupation, then, the individual may find the employing organization itself to be the most readily available job market; he is more likely to be visible there than elsewhere, on criteria which are sometimes unique to the organization; and much of his competence rests on knowledge of the particular organization and its environment.

Proposition 8.6: In the managerial technology, the inducements/contributions negotiation process rests on the individual's reputation for scarce abilities to solve organizational-rationality problems.

Jobs in this technology vary in the degree to which they afford opportunity for visibility and learning, and since career advancements tend to rest on moving higher within the organization, there is intense competition for jobs with large discretionary requirements. Individuals seek positive visibility and seek to influence the choice of assessment standards on which their performance is judged.

RECAPITULATION

Our basic argument has been that in preparing individuals for occupations, the social system provides them with a rather consistent set of aspirations, beliefs about causation, and standards. By locating jobs in technologies, on the other hand, organizations present individuals in a given occupation with patterned spheres of action. Since both sides of our accounting scheme—the individual and the situation presented to him—are patterned, we expect the resulting behavior to be patterned.

A job is both a unit in the organization and a unit in the career of an individual. Joining of the two is a result of a bargained agreement or inducements/contributions contract. In modern societies (Prop. 8.1), the content of that contract is determined through power processes. Contracts for jobs in routinized technologies (Prop. 8.2) are determined through collective bargaining, but at the contingent boundaries of the organization (Prop. 8.3), the contracts are determined by the power of the task-environment element and by the individual's ability to handle organizational dependence.

In intensive technologies (Prop. 8.4), individuals in early-ceiling occupations seek collective action to upgrade the occupation, but (Prop. 8.5) bargaining by those in late-ceiling occupations rests on visibility among occupational colleagues. In the managerial technology, the negotiation process (Prop. 8.6) rests on the individual's reputation for scarce abilities to solve problems of organizational rationality.

It is in the discretionary jobs—boundary-spanning, intensive, and managerial—that the political action of individuals is most likely to influence the continuous processes of organization and administration. We turn to a closer look at these in Chapter 9.

9

discretion and its exercise

If organizations under rationality norms must deal with uncertainty, the exercise of discretion by organizational members becomes a crucial element in organizational action. What can we say about members' orientations toward the exercise of discretion, and about the organization's efforts to channel or discipline it?

We have argued that the organization's need for discretion is differentially distributed within the organization and that this makes for differences in inducements/contributions bargaining (Chapter 8). We can add that there are obvious differences in the abilities of individuals to exercise discretion; both education and experience emphasize such differences and produce trained incapacity in other areas.

If both need for and ability to exercise discretion are differentially distributed, the problem is partly one of matching. This is most forcefully demonstrated at times of sudden mobilization, as in disaster (Thompson and Hawkes, 1962) or during war, when some individuals with well-developed discretionary abilities are inevitably subordinated to some who obviously lack such abilities. Yet even under such extreme conditions, organizations in societies fully geared to organizations can rely on institutionalized procedures and understandings to correct much of the initial mismatching; under norms of rationality, such organizations do indeed correct much of it. Discretionary jobs are usually arranged sequentially in career patterns so that those requiring larger amounts of discretion are filled after individuals have shown capacity to handle smaller amounts. Many discretionary jobs, moreover, require formal education or training which discourages or weeds out those most allergic to discretion.

Organizations in transitional societies may have less success in matching discretionary abilities with needs for discretion, for in such societies the educational institutions may not attach primacy to the preparation of decision makers, and only a minority may receive the appropriate education. Shortages of those equipped to exercise discretion result in a tendency for organizations in transitional societies to be centralized, bureaucratic, and inflexible. Frequently these complaints focus on the behavior of field offices as contrasted with headquarters (Gore, 1958). In contrast with organizations in fully geared societies, these characteristics appear irrational; in their contextual realities, however, they may be quite rational.

Motivation for Discretion

There are two quite distinct aspects to motivation for discretion: motivation to *occupy* discretionary jobs and motivation to *exercise* discretion in such jobs. Complex organizations seldom have serious problems in inducing individuals to occupy discretionary jobs, for both in societies geared to complex organizations and in transitional societies, prestige attaches to discretionary jobs, and organizations can reinforce this evaluation through the structure of rewards; i.e., by negotiating greater inducements for discretionary jobs (Jaques, 1956).

Motivation to exercise discretion is another matter and poses serious problems for all types of complex organizations. It seems clear that some individuals are more tolerant of risk and ambiguity than others (Atkinson, 1957), and also that such tolerance is more widely distributed in some societies than in others (Redfield, 1947; McClelland, 1961). Nevertheless we will work with a very simple assumption—*that individuals exercise discretion whenever they believe it is to their advantage to do so and seek to evade discretion on other occasions.*

This is a naïve version of a notion which has received considerable thought in economic theory; and more recently in game theory and statistical-decision theory (Von Neumann and Morgenstern, 1944; Luce and Raiffa, 1957) where such sophisticated concepts as "subjective probability," minimax," and "maximin" have appeared; and in sociology, (Homans, 1961; Blau, 1964).

Our naïve version does not say as much as the more sophisticated versions, but it has precisely the advantage that it gives us a starting point while committing us to very little. It does not, for example, commit us to any particular method of calculating advantage. Its principle significance for our purposes, however, is that it indicates that the exercise of discretion is not solely explained by personality factors nor by the objective situation. Our naïve assumption focuses on the *perceived relationship of negative and positive factors* in the situation, and it enables us to advance several plausible propositions about discretionary behavior in organizations.

Proposition 9.1: When the individual believes that his cause/effect resources are inadequate to the uncertainty, he will seek to evade discretion.

Here we are arguing that when uncertainty looms large in comparison with predictive ability, judgment is suspended and other techniques, resorted to. These may range from the flip of a coin, to quite elaborate devices for randomization, to the use of formulas (such as trend charts used by stock market tipsters), or to precedent. This situation may result from an incomplete technology (Chapter 2) or from lack of education or experience on the part of the individual. But it may also stem from contingency resulting from interdependence. Hence:

Proposition 9.1a: Organizations can thwart the exercise of discretion by establishing inappropriate structures.

When interdependence is so diffuse that the local job lacks command over the resources needed to carry out a discretionary commitment, we would expect the individual to evade discretion. This situation is sometimes referred to as "responsibility in excess of authority" (Prop. 7.5*b*).

We argued earlier (Chapter 5) that organizations would seek to localize interdependence and that, to the extent that this is achieved, the present proposition would be unnecessary. Realistically, we must observe that it is frequently impossible to localize interdependence to the degree necessary to ensure discretion at every discretionary point. More significant, perhaps, is the possibility that an organization comes to face a new set of circumstances before it adapts its structure to meet them (Chandler,

1962). Thus increasing complexity of technology or task environment may call for more flexibility and more discretion than the structure established at an earlier period can provide.

Proposition 9.2: The more serious the individual believes the consequences of error to be, the more he will seek to evade discretion.

Under these circumstances, pains are taken to seek and develop substitutes for judgment. Consequences of error may fall on others—such as clients—and cultural or professional norms frequently discourage individuals from "gambling with the lives of others," regardless of their recklessness with their own affairs. Thus faculty members in universities are tempted to employ objective tests which help to justify low grades that might affect student careers adversely. Trust officers responsible for managing other people's estates are reputed to be conservative. Personnel selection and placement tend to rely heavily on objective tests. Physicians faced with inconclusive diagnoses tend to err on the safe side (Fox, 1957; Scheff, 1963).

Often the reliance on formulas, precedent, or objective evidence or procedures does not eliminate the exercise of discretion, but rather eliminates some of the alternatives which might otherwise be considered.

Proposition 9.2a: Organizations can thwart the exercise of discretion by establishing inappropriate assessment criteria as bases for rewards and penalties.

If performance in discretionary jobs is evaluated in terms of adherence to rules (Prop. 7.8a) or in terms of quota filling (Prop. 7.8b), individuals in those jobs are discouraged from exercising discretion which would reduce their scores on such criteria (Blau, 1955).

Proposition 9.2b: Organizations can produce systematic bias in the exercise of discretion by assessing performance on multiple, incompatible criteria.

We must be careful in elaborating this proposition, for Cyert and March (1963) have pointed out that what appear to be incompatible goals or targets may in fact be rendered compatible by treating them sequentially, and Frank (1958) has shown that selective enforcement of multiple, competing standards is an organizational device for achieving adaptability by forcing executives to keep alert to what their superiors are emphasizing at a particular time. (This turns out to be a procedure for maintaining centralization of discretion.) We doubt, however, that there is escape from ambivalence for the unit which performs both technical-core and boundary-spanning roles, such as therapy-oriented prisons and mental hospitals, where custodial criteria are also inevitable.

We must not overlook the real possibility that individuals with low tolerance for ambiguity (Frenkel-Brunswik, 1949) may be motivated to occupy discretionary positions for which evasion is impossible.

Proposition 9.3: Complex organizations and their supporting social structures encourage some individuals to exercise organizational discretion at considerable personal sacrifice.

Where pressures for achievement are strong and achievement is measured by the exercise of discretion, some individuals with low tolerance for uncertainty will be swept into discretionary jobs. This situation, of course, is the source of the "executive-ulcer" hypothesis, and while this must remain merely a hypothesis in the absence of explanations of the psychosomatic mechanism and additional evidence, we can assert at a minimum that individuals in such situations may experience an entire career of discomfort.

We have indicated in Chapter 8 our belief that an action framework is useful in analyzing purposive behavior, and we have also suggested that the job can be viewed as a *sphere of action,* or arena, containing opportunities and constraints. The propositions offered above are consistent with those views, for we have argued that the individual will seek the most favorable results he perceives to be available, and that under some circumstances, these results come by evasion of discretion.

We have not predicted and cannot predict that all individuals in an organization will evade discretion or that all in certain kinds of positions will do so. We cannot predict in the abstract how an individual will behave within his sphere of action, for our framework insists that his behavior is conditioned by his beliefs about causation, the level of his aspirations, and his norms. Lacking information on these variables, we can only indicate the kinds of temptations organizations sometimes build into certain jobs, and the direction which behavior is likely to take if the individual yields to those temptations.

Our consideration so far is based on the simplest case of inducements/contributions relationship, where in exchange for consequences favorable to the organization, the individual receives rewards. We now need to consider the fact that alternatives sometimes have compound or multiple consequences.

MULTIPLE CONSEQUENCES OF DISCRETION

Alternatives available to the organization member may have direct consequences for him quite apart from their consequences for the organization and from the rewards and penalties offered by the organization as part of the inducements/contributions contract (Thompson, 1962). The most obvious examples are those where (1) individuals are tempeted to exercise discretion while the organizational definition of the job permits no discretion and (2) individuals employ criteria which officially are not accepted. For convenience, we will refer to this as *deviant discretion.*

Proposition 9.4: Organizations seek to guard against deviant discretion by policing methods.

Quantity and quality standards are characteristic of routinized jobs in complex organizations; but, in addition, organizations typically develop procedures for testing compliance with rules and for detecting misappropriation of organization resources, favoritism, and bribery. Temptations in these directions seem to be inevitable wherever organizations flourish, for in such societies the social structure presses individuals to achieve, while highly prescribed jobs set limits to the speed or absolute levels of achievement. (On relation between means and ends, and individual adaptations, see Merton, 1957c, and Cohen, 1965.)

The discrepancy between pressure to achieve and feasibility of achievement undoubtedly varies from one society to another and from time to time within a society. On the whole, we would expect deviant discretion to be a greater problem in societies not fully geared to complex organizations than in societies which possess the appropriate supporting institutions, where notions of rational-legal bases for authority (Weber, 1947) and of career reinforce employment contracts, and professional societies establish norms for discretionary occupations. Bribery, for example, is usually considered a scandal in the society geared to complex organizations; it may be an accepted procedure in societies which have not made the transition.

While the amount of deviant discretion by members of organizations is undoubtedly a variable, the potential is inevitable wherever organizations exist and leads us to expect that organizations everywhere, subjected to rationality norms, will employ policing tactics. This in turn leads us to expect an aura of distrust on both sides, of organizations by members in prescribed jobs and of the latter by organizations. We would expect policing activities and mutual suspicions to be more prevalent in organizations with a preponderance of routinized jobs than in more dynamic organizations, and we would expect policing and mutual suspicions to be stronger during transitions than after the society has become geared to complex organizations. Suspicions, however, may linger after the reality has been reduced.

Now we have indicated that organizations have problems when individuals in discretionary jobs fail to exercise discretion, and that they also have problems when individuals in routinized jobs do exercise discretion. But we would expect that in the more complicated organizations, the difficulties regarding the exercise of discretion tend to fall in the more subtle, gray areas between those extremes. Characteristically, the problems arise because it is difficult to determine whether a choice is more beneficial to the organization than to the individual, or vice versa; i.e., whether choices enlarge or protect the action sphere of the individual and whether this is given primacy over enhancement of the organization's interest.

We can assume that where alternatives are perceived to have equal consequences for the organization, the individual will select that alternative which favors his sphere of action—enlarging it if possible, or defending it. But reality introduces the complication that alternatives seldom have equal consequences or that their consequences can only be estimated. At this point the variable of standards or norms becomes crucial (Chapter 8); we cannot predict in the abstract what an individual will do, but we can indicate the nature of the temptations placed before him.

Proposition 9.5: Where work loads exceed capacity and the individual has options, he is tempted to select tasks which promise to enhance his scores on assessment criteria.

When work overloads exist, effort must be rationed; the individual is not exercising discretion over whether to work or not. He is simply selecting the criteria for rationing—criteria which enable him to amass a larger number of successful tasks or a higher percentage of successful "treatments"; or to make sure that his efforts are noticed by those who control rewards or, more importantly, those with whom inducements/contributions contracts can be renegotiated.

We would expect caseworkers, for example, to focus attention on those cases or clients which appear likely to be resolved successfully, quickly, and with visibility for the individual (Thompson, 1962).

Proposition 9.6: Where work loads or resource supplies fluctuate, the individual is tempted to stockpile.

The practice of "banking" a supply of finished parts as insurance against a bad day was reported in the Hawthorne study (Roethlisberger and Dickson, 1939) and has been widely observed in other settings. Leniency by supervisors in enforcing rules is a way of creating an obligation for subordinates to respond energetically in emergencies (Gouldner, 1954); similar findings have been reported of guards and prisoners (Sykes, 1956).

This proposition seems to us to be a more plausible explanation for "empire building" than the usual explanations of "hunger for power" or of rewards being directly proportional to the size of the activity. It is not unusual for essential activities, such as fire protection, to be staffed for peak loads and thus to appear oversupplied or overmanned during off-peak periods. By the same reasoning, we would expect the individual who believes his rewards to be dependent on performance under extreme conditions, to seek insurance by acquiring manpower or supplies equal to anticipated peak loads. Hoarding reduces the individual's future dependence on others.

Proposition 9.7: Where alternatives are present, the individual is tempted to report successes and suppress evidence of failures.

Distortion of organizational records is a widespread phenomenon. Frequently those receiving reports or records are as aware of discrepancies as those making reports, having practiced the same or similar deceptions themselves. We would expect "favorable biases" to appear wherever rewards are influenced by records, and alternative ways of reporting are available; we would not expect other than random errors on matters which do not affect the distribution of rewards.

Under some conditions individuals are induced to falsify reports completely, but the more subtle and perhaps more serious cases occur where estimates or judgments of accomplishment are involved. In a great many instances the outcomes of action do not fall within periods covered by organizational assessments, and one must resort to projections. In other cases, the ramifications of action are not fully determined because cause/effect understanding is incomplete. In either event, our expectation is that the individual will emphasize that evidence or estimate which resounds to his credit and will deemphasize the damaging evidence or estimate.

Now we have indicated our belief that individuals with discretion will be tempted to select easy tasks or amass resources for their tasks and will seek biased scores on assessment criteria. These propositions refer to discretion within the parameters of the established job. To the extent that favorable visibility in the job may earn the individual a better job, these forms of discretion may have consequences for job parameters. But that is indirect, and we also need to consider the possibilities that individuals in discretionary jobs may exercise discretion to influence favorably the parameters of their jobs. The most often voiced example of this is the complaint that central executives of corporations may gain sufficient stockholder proxies to vote themselves higher salaries, bonuses, or other inducements. The more subtle possibilities, however, lie in re-arrangements of organizational structure, the installation of new assessment criteria and procedures, or revision of resource-allocation procedures.

DISCRETION AND POLITICS

Positions containing discretion over structure, assessment systems, resource allocations, or domain commitments will be referred to as *highly discretionary positions*. In all but the simplest organizations, the exercise of discretion in such a position may also enhance or threaten the action spheres of others in nearby positions. When an organization attains any significant degree of complexity, it also contains a considerable amount of interdependence among its highly discretionary jobs; i.e., decisions in each can have consequences for the action spheres of others in the group, and can in turn be affected by decisions taken elsewhere in the group. It is here that we would expect to find developed political processes in operation.

Several assumptions about incumbents of such positions seem reasonable: (1) individuals in highly discretionary jobs have high aspirations and are therefore interested in favorable spheres of action; (2) individuals in highly discretionary jobs are not reluctant to exercise discretion; and (3) individuals in highly discretionary jobs have developed political skills.

Proposition 9.8: Individuals in highly discretionary jobs seek to maintain power equal to or greater than their dependence on others in the organization.

The rational-model version of this proposition is old and well known, as "authority equal to responsibility." We have converted it into a natural-system version, thus recognizing that individuals may maintain or enhance their positions regardless of the official, authorized positions they hold. We are thus able to "explain" those situations in organizations in which it is said that there is a "power behind the throne," an "invisible government," or a "kitchen cabinet." Our version has an additional advantage. Under the rational-model approach, the individual's only redress is to petition through official channels for a correction of his situation. Under the version here, the individual has more possibilities.

Proposition 9.8a: When the power of an individual in a highly discretionary job is less than his dependence, he will seek a coalition.

Coalition behavior has received considerable attention in recent years in small-group research (Thibaut and Kelley, 1959), in game theory (for example, Von Neumann and Morgenstern, 1944), and in the behavioral theory of the firm (March, 1962; Cyert and March, 1963). Coalition behavior is undoubtedly of major importance to our understanding of complex organizations. Generally, it is assumed that coalitions are formed under conditions of conflict and high aspirations. These are important instances, but we also need to recognize that coalition behavior can be defensive as well as aggressive.

Proposition 9.8b: Individuals representing precarious values in the organization become junior partners in organizational coalitions.

Clark's (1956) pioneering study of an activity which was not highly regarded by the dominant coalition has focused attention on the problem of those responsible for low-priority activities. Zald (1962) reports a similar position for school principals and teachers in correctional institutions, where training was not central to the definition of institutional philosophy.

We would expect such individuals, out of defensive considerations, to be active candidates for coalition agreements.

Proposition 9.8c: To increase their power in organizations, individuals in highly discretionary jobs may form coalitions with essential elements of the task environment.

We are thus viewing coalitions as *linkages* of competences or abilities which occur when two or more individuals in discretionary positions believe that their abilities to satisfy organizational dependencies are greater in combination than singly, and where the results of increased power can be shared. Whether coalition members are all members of the organization or include representatives of the task environment depends on the location of abilities and on the location of organizational dependencies. In any event,

Proposition 9.9: Changes in organizational dependencies threaten some coalitions and make new ones possible.

If we are correct that coalitions are viable only at points where the organization is vulnerable—i.e., where the organization has important dependencies—then any change in these is going to bring into question the foundations of the coalition. Structural rearrangements which relocate interdependencies, design changes which reduce reliance on the environment, or changes in the nature of the task environment are thus of major concern to those involved in organizational coalitions. Even those not actively engaged in coalition behavior may, of course, have a stake in such changes. Hence we would expect individuals in highly discretionary jobs to be concerned about organizational goals.

ORGANIZATIONAL GOALS

There is obvious danger in reifying the abstraction "organization" by asserting that it, the abstraction, has goals or desires (Cyert and March, 1963; Perrow, 1961; Simon, 1964). There is little to be gained, however, by swinging to the other extreme of insisting that the goals of an organization are somehow the accumulated goals of its individual members.

The goal question was sidestepped earlier (Chapter 3), and we have been able to consider a number of important aspects of organizational action using the notion of domain. That tactic has had the advantage of pointing up the relevance of task environment, together with technology, in determining the limits of possible action for the organization.

The notion of domain, however, is timeless, while the notion of goal has an undeniable future dimension. We use "goal" to refer only to some imagined state of affairs which may conceivably be attained or approached (if not finite) at some future time. Even though domain considerations press on the organization at any point in time and set limits for the organization, a different domain posture may always be imagined for the future.

It seems reasonable to consider goals *for* an organization as *intended future domains* for the organization. Goals for the organization will usually be multiple and may be held by individuals or categories having no affiliation with the organization. In this way clientele may seek a different sort of service from the organization; investors may seek a more profitable or safer domain for the organization; members of the environment may seek to define the domain as illegitimate; or members of different departments within the organization may have conflicting views of desired future domains. Considering goals as intended future domains has the utility that it allows us to consider that nonmembers may have goals for the organization and, in fact, may be quite active in trying to change an organization's domains.

But we can also consider goals *of* the organization, or organizational goals, as the *future domains intended by those in the dominant coalition.* Almost inevitably this includes organizational members, but it may also incorporate significant outsiders. It is doubtful if, in correctional institutions or mental hospitals, the therapeutic goal could become the organizational goal without the help of nonmembers. Alone, the therapeutic faction in such organizations probably cannot wrest control from the custodial faction. If, following a reform movement, the nonmember elements withdraw from participation in the coalition, custodial forces may be able to regain control. This may help explain what appears to be vacillation in such fields.

The view of organizational goals presented here overcomes both of the traditional problems; we have not reified the organization, nor have we simply added the preferences of all members. In this view, organizational goals are established by individuals—but interdependent individuals who collectively have sufficient control of organizational resources to commit them in certain directions and to withhold them from others.

This view of organizational goals is entirely consistent with, and indeed is basically derived from, that of Cyert and March (1963), who insist that "side payments, far from being the incidental distribution of a fixed, transferable booty, represent the central process of goal specification. That is, a significant number of these payments are in the form of policy commitments" (p. 30).

This view also gives us a way of plausibly explaining the often noted tendency of organizations to seek survival and growth. So long as the organization presents favorable spheres of action to individuals in highly discretionary jobs, we have a strong motivation for them to avoid decisions which would end those spheres of action. If we make the additional assumptions that generations will usually overlap in the dominant coalition, we have the necessary bases for expecting perpetuation of the organization beyond the effective life span of an individual.

POWER STRUCTURE VARIATIONS

If power in an organization rests on ability to solve dependency problems for the organization (Crozier, 1964), what can we say about the structure of power within an organization?

Proposition 9.10: The more sources of uncertainty or contingency for the organization, the more bases there are for power and the larger the number of political positions in the organization.

The more complicated organizations (as defined in Chapter 6) should therefore exhibit more organizational politics than the less complicated ones, for complexity means more or deeper interdependencies and therefore more points of contingency. Similarly, we would expect the organization which is open to the environment at only a few points to contain fewer political positions than the organization facing a heterogeneous environment on a variety of fronts. Thus, in proportion to the total membership of the organization, we would expect the hospital or university to have a wider political base than the army division or the manufacturing division of an industrial firm.

Proposition 9.10a: Decentralization dilutes the power structure by creating more power positions but limiting the organization's dependence on each one.

In terms of Proposition 6.4, decentralization segments the major components of an organization and arranges the segments into self-sufficient clusters. Since each cluster has its own domain, dependence tends to be confined to that domain, and thus the ability of an individual to handle that dependence is of limited usefulness to the organization. [Some of the administrative, as contrasted to efficiency, consequences of decentralization are brought out by Wilson (1966).]

Proposition 9.11: The more dynamic the technology and task environment, the more rapid the political processes in the organization and the more frequent the changes in organizational goals.

Since we believe that changes in interdependence—internally resulting from technological developments, and externally based on changes in task-environment elements—produce changes in the political positions in the organization, it follows that the more changeable these interdependencies, the more changeable the coalitions involved. Where the necessary inputs are widely available in the environment, those responsible for obtaining them will have little basis for power in the organization. As those same inputs become scarce, we will expect the individual to become more powerful in the organization. This should apply to personnel activities, financial responsibilities, capital equipment, or raw materials, as well as to activities associated with output disposal. The reverse should also hold, that as an activity loses its problematic character, the individual responsible for it will lose power.

In these speculations we are assuming that members of the dominant coalition perceive changes in technology or task environment and thus perceive the need or the opportunity to adjust the power structure. We can expect the task environment to signal, more or less rapidly, the emergence of new dependencies and thus the basis for new power positions in the dominant coalition. However, we cannot assume the reverse. When a formerly important dependency becomes more easily solved, there is no reason to expect that this fact will be called to the attention of others in the dominant coalition. Indeed, the individual whose position has been eroded may not perceive that fact until he is challenged. Since we believe that individuals in the dominant coalition generally have well-developed political skills, we would expect shifts in the power base to be perceived rather quickly by at least some individuals in the dominant coalition, and therefore we would expect rather rapid adaptability under norms of rationality.

There is an additional possibility, however, which can cause serious lags in the ability of the organization to adapt its goals to the realities of changing technologies or task environments.

Proposition 9.12: When organizations commit future control over resources in exchange for present solutions to contingencies, they create limitations on their abilities to adapt to future change of technologies or task environments.

Most generally this takes the form of appointment of the competent individual to a permanent, or tenured, position—as director, manager, dean, vice president, or superintendent—with no provision for termination short of death or retirement. Many such appointments, of course, remain beneficial to the organization in the sense that the scope of the position remains important to the organization, and the individual remains competent. But if changes in technology or task environment call for new or adjusted competence in the position, and the individual fails to match it, the organization may be crippled or required to build around that individual. To the extent that he can retain jurisdiction over resources, however, he cannot be ignored. This is a situation which frequently results in internal feuding climaxed by a showdown struggle for power.

RECAPITULATION

Organizations must find individuals with capacity to occupy important discretionary positions, but the organization must also induce their discretionary behavior. When (Prop. 9.1) the individual believes that his cause/effect resources are inadequate to the uncertainty, he will seek to evade discretion, and organizations can thwart the exercise of discretion through inappropriate structures. The more serious the individual believes the consequences of error to be (Prop. 9.2), the more he will seek to evade discretion, and the use of inappropriate assessment methods can thwart the exercise of discretion.

The exercise of discretion on behalf of the organization may entail considerable personal sacrifice for the individual, but on the other hand, organizations employ (Prop. 9.4) policing methods to guard against unwanted discretion. Where options remain for the individual, and work loads exceed capacity (Prop. 9.5), he is likely to select tasks which promise to enhance his scores on assessment criteria; where workloads or resource supplies fluctuate (Prop. 9.6), he is likely to stockpile; and where alternatives are present (Prop. 9.7), he is tempted to report successes and suppress evidence of failures.

Highly discretionary jobs are involved in political processes, and (Prop. 9.8) individuals in such jobs seek to maintain power equal to or greater than their dependence. If necessary for this purpose (Prop. 9.8a), they participate in coalitions. Therefore, changes in organizational dependencies (Prop. 9.9) threaten some coalitions and make new ones possible. The more sources of uncertainty for the organization (Prop. 9.10), the larger the number of political positions in the organization; and the more dynamic the technology and task environment (Prop. 9.11), the more rapid the political processes. However, limitations on the adaptability to such changes can arise if (Prop. 9.12) organizations commit future control over resources in exchange for present solutions to contingencies.

We have now considered where discretion lies in complex organizations, the motivations for exercising it, and some of the consequences. In the following chapter we turn to an analysis of how discretionary choices are arrived at.

10

the control of complex organizations

We have asserted, with Cyert and March (1963), that organizational goals are established through coalition behavior. We have done so on grounds that organizations are interdependent with task-environment elements and that organizational components are also interdependent with one another. Unilateral action is not compatible with interdependence. The "pyramid" headed by the single all-powerful individual has become a symbol of complex organizations, but through historical and misleading accident. The all-powerful chief can maintain such control only to the extent that he is not dependent on others within his organization; and this is a situation of *modest complexity*, not one of a high degree of complexity.

We might expect to find concentrated power within certain units of some highly complex organizations, perhaps in the technical cores of those organizations which have standardized, repetitive activities, and which have succeeded in isolating or buffering those activities from environmental fluctuations (Chapter 2). The appearance of omnipotence may also occur in the small organization whose resources are assured or supplied by a parent organization—routine governmental bureaus, subordinate military units, wholly owned corporate subsidiaries—provided input and output problems are relatively smooth. In such cases, of course, the individual who appears omnipotent within the organization is highly dependent on his external sources of support, and the pyramid concept is in important ways misleading.

The omnipotent-individual assumption is consistent with the rational-model approach to organizations, but is negated under any one of the following conditions, all of which are compatible with the natural-system model:

(1) When complexity of the technology or technologies exceeds the comprehension of the individual. This does not necessarily have anything to do with the individual's intelligence, but rather with his experience. Conceivably the university president, hospital chief executive, or corporation chairman is intelligent enough to earn his spurs in any of the disciplines contained within his organization, but this requires more than one lifetime. At an earlier period, the combat unit in military organization was commanded by the officer who had demonstrated his capacity to perform all aspects of the technology well; with the development of electronically controlled weapons systems, for example, the individual's knowledge of some aspects must be limited to familiarity (Janowitz, 1959).

(2) When resources required exceed the capacity of the individual to acquire. Again we can cite the modern university president, the community hospital administrator, or the corporation.

(3) When the organization faces contingencies on more fronts than the individual is able to keep under surveillance. Thus the military commander who prior to battle runs a tight operation may lose much of his control in a complicated battle. Similarly, the organization which decides to expand and diversify may thereby be forced to enlarge its dominant coalition (Chapter 9).

How large, relative to the remainder of the organization, the dominant coalition needs to be depends on several factors which we can best consider after we have reviewed the nature of control within the organization. Simon (1957a) has shown that such control is achieved through manipulation at each hierarchical level of the decision premises used by lower levels. If this is true, then the nature and stability of the dominant coalition must depend on its ability to manipulate decision premises, and we now need a scheme which will enable us to differentiate among decision situations.

Decision issues always involve two major dimensions: (1) beliefs about cause/effect relations and (2) preferences regarding possible outcomes (Thompson and Tuden, 1959). This does not mean that both dimensions are consciously considered in every discretionary situation, but simply that both are operating at some level. These are the *basic variables* of decision.

Either variable can take on a large range of values, but to keep our discussion within bounds, we will dichotomize each and proceed as if there could either be certainty or uncertainty regarding causation, and certainty or uncertainty regarding outcome preferences (Thompson, 1964). This gives four types of decision issues:

Preferences regarding possible outcomes

		Certainty	*Uncertainty*
Beliefs about cause/effect relations	*Certain*		
	Uncertain		

It seems clear that each type of decision issue calls for a different strategy. Where there is certainty regarding both causation and outcome preferences, we will speak of a *computational strategy* for decision making. Although it might seem that no decision is required under such circumstances, if data are voluminous for formulas are intricate, the solution is not obvious. This is what Simon (1960) has termed a "programmed decision," and it is for such issues that electronic computers have been most widely employed.

Where outcome preferences are clear but cause/effect relationships are uncertain, we will refer to the *judgmental strategy* for decision making. Where the situation is reversed and there is certainty regarding cause/effect but uncertainty regarding outcome preferences, the issue can be regarded as calling for a *compromise strategy* for decision making.

Finally, where there is uncertainty on both dimensions, we will speak of the *inspirational strategy* for decision making, if indeed any decision is forthcoming.

CONTROL OF DECISION PREMISES

Now if the dominant coalition of an organization can specify for component units both the cause/effect beliefs to be employed and the relevant hierarchy of outcomes to be preferred (or *utility scale*), then the units involved may employ a *computational strategy,* and the only questions revolve around accuracy of data; here full and accurate communication is of great concern and positively valued. Hence if each organizational unit takes as its decisional premises the outcome preferences and the cause/effect belief system specified by the next higher level in the hierarchy, the organizational structure conforms to Weber's (1947) bureaucratic model, and the *dominant coalition* is indeed omnipotent. The coalition in this case may very well be an individual.

But in reality there are often constraints on the coalition's ability to specify either variable.

Constraints on Cause/Effect Premises

The most obvious reason for the inability of a dominant coalition to specify the cause/effect beliefs to be used in decision is incompleteness in the existing knowledge. Although complex organizations are not established when knowledge is totally absent, they frequently do operate with incomplete knowledge (Chapter 2). This would be true, for example, of organizations working on the edges of established knowledge, such as new areas of surgery, new phases in a national space program, or basic research. Even though all variables known to be pertinent are under unilateral control and may be specified by the dominant coalition, imperfections or gaps in knowledge call for the judgmental strategy.

A second and perhaps more pervasive constraint on the dominant coalition occurs when the object worked on is itself dynamic, for here some of the pertinent variables are not unilaterally under control of the organization (Thompson, 1962). Thus the outcome of an educational program may hinge in large measure on the student's desire to learn, and therapeutic programs designed to modify basic personality or character structures are greatly affected by cooperation or antagonism of the human targets.

Still a third type of constraint on the coalition's ability to dictate cause/effect relationships arises from competition between the organization and others. Competition (Thompson and McEwen, 1958) is a situation in which the decision unit and at least one other seek to influence the behavior of a third party; e.g., the television network's fall programming. Here the decision unit retains unilateral control of its preference hierarchy but must behave toward prospective customers, suppliers, or "judges" in light of its expectations about the behavior of both rivals and prospects. Where outcomes are in part determined by the behavior of others, cause/effect relationships are uncertain, and this leads us to expect use of the judgmental strategy.

We indicated in Chapter 9 that the individual in a highly discretionary position who was able to handle crucial contingencies for the organization could demand a place in the dominant coalition. Several things appear to follow:

Proposition 10.1: The more numerous the areas in which the organization must rely on the judgmental decision strategy, the larger the dominant coalition.

This is essentially a restatement of Proposition 9.10, but in terms of decision strategies.

Proposition 10.1a: The less perfect the core technology, the more likely it will be represented in the dominant coalition.

Proposition 10.1b: The more heterogeneous the task environment, the larger the number of task-environment specialists in the dominant coalition.

Under these propositions, we would expect to find the small dominant coalition, perhaps the single individual, in organizations repeating standardized technological activities to produce standardized results for standardized customers or clients. Examples would be Dill's (1958) Alpha, a Norwegian firm in the clothing and textile industry, in contrast to his Beta, which imported foreign manufactures for resale, did some assembly and manufacturing work, and performed a wide variety of engineering, installation, and maintenance services. Other examples would include utility organizations—heating, electricity, water, etc.—where the most significant contingencies are likely to be financial (for capital investment) and regulatory; i.e., the actions of regulatory commissions or of legislatures.

Proposition 10.2: As areas within the organization shift from characteristically computational to characteristically judgmental decision strategies, the dominant coalition will expand to include their representatives, and vice versa.

For example, as hospitals shifted from custodial organizations for the dying (where computational decision processes were appropriate) to therapeutic organizations (where judgmental decision processes were appropriate), representatives of the medical profession gained power in the dominant coalition, in spite of the fact that frequently the medical staff is not incorporated into organization membership (Lentz, 1957; Perrow, 1965). We would expect to find the prison shift from custodial to therapeutic goals accompanied by enlargement of the dominant coalition to include professionals (Cressy, 1965; Grusky, 1959; Zald, 1962).

We would also expect shifts through time in the composition of the dominant coalition in manufacturing firms. Where production is on a custom basis, perhaps in the early stages of the firm, we would expect technical leaders to be important in the coalition; but as experience permits perfection and mass production, we would expect those positions to be dropped from the dominant coalition. (This does not necessarily mean that a given individual will be dropped, for he may have other bases for power. The inventor may be powerful initially because of his technological capability, and later because of his patent rights or his financial capacity.) During periods of input scarcity, leaders of input components would have bases for membership in the dominant coalition, but would lose these when the necessary inputs become abundant. Similarly, when customers are clamoring for the product, sales executives have little basis for membership in the dominant coalition, but when competition is brisk, their power should rise (Thompson, 1964).

Constraints on Outcome-Preference Premises

Members of a dominant coalition are, of course, free to prefer anything; but for purposes of control over the organization, the effective preferences are those for which there is an instrumentally rational approach (Chapter 2). Only those preferences which conceivably are *outcomes* of possible action by the organization are therefore relevant, and such outcome possibilities are constrained in several ways.

When the core technology of an organization must be employed on dynamic human objects, the outcome is in part determined by those human objects; and if they hold opposing outcome preferences, some compromise is likely. Thus in prisons with therapeutic objectives, some compromise seems inevitable, for conflicting outcome preferences of prisoners force the prison to add custody as an outcome preference. A similar conflict among objectives often occurs in mental hospitals, although to the extent that tranquilizing drugs render patients cooperative, therapeutic measures may gain priority over custodial ones. This matter of compromise also shows up clearly in public education, and marks one major difference between schools whose students are "motivated" and those whose students are not.

A second constraint on the dominant coalition's ability to manipulate premises about outcome preferences occurs when needed inputs are hard to get. Whether the necessary inputs be client referrals (Levine and White, 1961), materials, legitimation (Selznick, 1949), or other, those on whom the organization is dependent may hold veto power over some possible goals for the organization. Such external constraints on outcome preferences are particularly felt when the task-environment element has power to grant or withhold accreditation and professional recognition. Where such power exists, the organization may indeed be forced to compromise on or delimit its outcome preferences.

DYNAMICS OF ORGANIZATIONAL CONTROL

An organization's dominant coalition is by no means a static, fixed item. We have hinted that long-term changes can occur, but we must also observe that a coalition inevitably is *in process*. The rapidity of movement and the ease with which it can be distinguished are, of course, variables; but it is evidence of conflict within the coalition that emphasizes that in the last analysis a coalition is a process, not an entity.

Proposition 10.3: Potential for conflict within the dominant coalition increases with interdependence of the members (and the areas they represent or control).

As issues arise within the coalition, possible solutions may call for rearrangement of the inducements/contributions balance which holds the coalition together, and this possibility clearly carries conflict potential with it. Since we would expect the decision process to involve all affected members of the coalition, the wider the interdependence net, the wider we would expect the possibilities for conflict to be.

Proposition 10.4: Potential for conflict within the dominant coalition increases as external forces require internal compromise on outcome preferences.

Here we have in mind especially those organizations which are committed to therapeutic goals and technologies, but are also forced to apply resources to custody. This condition, we would expect, builds into the dominant coalition two factions with competing claims on resources, decision premises, etc. We would expect such organizations typically to show conflict within the dominant coalition.

Proposition 10.5: Potential for conflict within the dominant coalition increases with the variety of professions incorporated.

Since we believe that professional members of the organization develop identifications with their profession which may place constraints on organizational outcome preferences (Caplow and McGee, 1958; Gouldner, 1957–58; Hughes, 1958; Marcson, 1960), it follows that the larger the variety of such possible constraints, the more likely an issue is to call into question the inducements/contributions balance underlying the dominant coalition at any particular time. Moreover, when the organization incorporates larger numbers of professionals, the tendency is for them to insist that decision premises be set only by professionals, and this generates potential for conflict within the dominant coalition between professionals and others. Uneasiness seems to be characteristic of relations between professionals and lay administrators in research organizations, hospitals, universities, social welfare agencies, and schools. When ideologies deny legitimation to laymen, but the realities of interdependence require that laymen be incorporated in the dominant coalition, conflict is likely.

COALITION MANAGEMENT

We have said that several forces are particularly important in shaping the dominant coalition and its behavior in the organization. What would happen if we combined those least consistent with the rational model into a single organization? Suppose we force the organization to employ the judgmental decision strategy in multiple areas, thus making for a large coalition; we place the organization in a heterogeneous task environment and make it dependent, thus enlarging the number of task-environment specialists in the dominant coalition; and we make the organization highly interdependent, thus building in a conflict potential. Do we now have a coalition so divided as to immobilize the organization? Are there no offsetting factors? Is there no power to ride herd on warring factions?

Consider the modern university, which probably fits the above description as well as anything we could build. It employs a wide variety of professionals to exercise judgment frequently. It is highly dependent on many different aspects of a large and dynamic task environment. True, it localizes much of its interdependence (Chapter 5) in departments, institutes, schools, colleges, and divisions; yet anyone familiar with the modern university will recognize that research and teaching demands require considerable coordination which is not contained in the usual clusterings.

The power base of the university is quite wide, relative to organizations of similar size, officially fanning out on some types of issues to include all members of the faculty; and even on more subtle matters to include not only presidents, vice presidents, deans and department chairmen, but also senior faculty members in a large number of areas of the university. Unilateral action by a university president on significant issues is relatively rare.

But in spite of the fact that the university fits the notion of a large and diverse coalition and that it exists in a dynamic task environment which regularly poses significant issues, the modern university is not simply a battleground for the continual conflict within coalitions. Some universities appear to be, at times, but they are remarkable and remarked about. Moreover, in spite of a wide distribution of power in the coalition, the president of the modern university frequently holds considerable power in his own right.

The case of the modern university, at least as sketched here, raises several important questions. How, when it faces serious issues continuously, can the organization with a diverse and large dominant coalition get anything done other than coalition infighting? How can an individual be powerful in the face of widely distributed power and the absence of unilateral power?

Proposition 10.6: When power is widely distributed, an *inner circle* emerges to conduct coalition business.

This inner-circle arrangement may be formalized, with elected or appointed delegates representing factions or categories, but perhaps more often it emerges informally, implicitly, tacitly. In the large university, for example, no one individual (president, dean, or other) can renegotiate coalitions dealing simultaneously with 500 or 1,000 faculty members plus perhaps 25 to 50 board members and other necessary parties. There will usually be formalized channels—the faculty as a legislative chamber, or a council or senate of representatives of the faculty, and an executive committee of the board—to consider issues and exercise discretion or express preferences. But when issues require swift action, the president may attain faculty approval simply by checking the sentiments of half a dozen faculty members, each well known, respected, and trusted by a different, major segment of the faculty.

Whether such individuals act formally, as elected or appointed representatives, or informally, they are *reflecting* the power of those for whom they speak. They may indeed gain a measure of power with respect to the president, chancellor, or board of regents by being in the inner circle; but their ability to maintain such power rests, we would think, on their accuracy and honesty in reflecting the beliefs and preferences of their colleagues. We would expect, then, that any suspicion that members of the inner circle were using this position for personal gain at the expense of the larger coalition would immediately eliminate the inner circle from power.

Proposition 10.7: The organization with dispersed bases of power is immobilized unless there exists an effective inner circle.

Both judgmental and compromise decision processes are feasible in pluralistic situations (Thompson and Tuden, 1959), but with large numbers, only the judgmental strategy is feasible, and then only under majority rule. The subtle processes of compromise cannot work with large numbers, and in the absence or failure of an inner circle, the dominant coalition must cling to the existing balances of inducements and contributions, for there is no mechanism for renegotiation.

Proposition 10.8: When power is widely dispersed, compromise issues can be ratified but cannot be decided by the dominant coalition in toto.

The situation is insightfully analyzed by Stryker's (1963) consideration of the university departmental faculty faced with the issue of curriculum revision. Here each member's work load, subject matter, and perhaps career chances are at stake. Moreover, under the usual professional norms in the United States, curriculum decisions should be made in the interests of the student and the university, not in the interests of the individual faculty member. Yet the inducements/contributions balance of each faculty member must be renegotiated, and the resulting solutions must simultaneously mesh into an overall result. Stryker points out that attempts to revise curricula in faculty meetings fall flat. Where revisions are accomplished, it is by an individual or small committee which can meet informally and individually with each member until the necessary series of compromises appear to mesh. At this point, the faculty vote is not a decision but formal acknowledgment or ratification of the renegotiation.

Management of the Coalition

We have argued that in the highly complex organization, power is dispersed. We have argued that for the organization to be decisive and dynamic, the dispersed power must be reflected in and exercised through an inner circle. Have we thus defined such organizations as inevitably lacking a central power symbol, a recognized leader? Certainly we are implying that unilateral power cannot fall to one man in such organizations. Yet we know that an individual can "cast the long shadow" over an organization which without doubt has widely dispersed power.

Proposition 10.9: In the organization with dispersed power, the central power figure is the individual who can manage the coalition.

Hawkes' (1961) study of the psychiatric executive provides the clue. Although psychiatric hospitals and universities do differ in significant respects, both are among the most complex organizations, face both judgmental and compromise issues regularly, rely to a great extent on professionals, and face dynamic task environments. (Our interest is less in the hospital and the university than in organizations which meet those conditions.)

Hawkes observed in the psychiatric case that the organization undertook obligations in three major sectors of the task environment: the medical sector, the patient-population sector, and the legal-financial sector. Necessary inputs were received from each, and obligations were incurred toward each. In effecting the three "contracts," Hawkes observed, only the chief executive had access to all three sectors. Psychiatrists had access to both the patient population and the medical environment, but were dependent on the chief executive for representation with the legal-financial sector. In our terms, only the chief executive could bring the necessary financial-legal elements of the task environment into the coalition.

It seems clear, then, that in the highly complex organization, an individual can be powerful, can symbolize the power of the organization, and can exercise significant leadership; but we would predict, as in the case of the inner circle, that he can do so only with the consent and approval of the dominant coalition. Thus the highly complex organization is not the place for the dictator or commander to emerge. In the highly complex organization, in our opinion, neither the central power figure nor the inner circle (nor their combination) can reverse the direction of organizational movement at will.

For rapid, abrupt adaptation of an organization to a new set of circumstances, the bureaucracy is undoubtedly "tops"; and it frequently is observed that with a well-developed bureaucratic apparatus as in England, France, or the United States, shifts in governments and hence in policy can cause hardly a missed beat in the bureaucratic rhythm. In these situations, a chief executive can substitute one decision premise for another, indoctrinate, and enforce. But the administrative process calls for something else in the highly complex organization.

Without the "superb politician," metropolitan school systems, urban governments, universities, mental hospitals, social work systems, and similar complex organizations would be immobilized.

RECAPITULATION

Although the pyramid headed by an all-powerful individual has been a symbol of organizations, such omnipotence is possible only in simple situations where perfected technologies and bland task environments make computational decision processes feasible. Where technology is incomplete or the task environment heterogeneous, the judgmental decision strategy is required and control is vested in a dominant coalition. The more numerous the areas needing judgment, the (Prop. 10.1) larger the dominant coalition, and as areas within the organization shift from characteristically computational to characteristically judgmental decision strategies (Prop. 10.2), the dominant coalition will expand to include their representatives.

Potential for conflict within the dominant coalition (Prop. 10.3) increases with interdependence of the members and the areas they represent, and (Prop. 10.4) as external forces require internal compromise on outcome preferences. Potential for conflict also increases (Prop. 10.5) with the variety of professions incorporated in the organization.

When such forces result in a wide distribution of power and therefore in a large dominant coalition, coalition business (Prop. 10.6) is conducted by an inner circle. Without an effective inner circle, such an organization (Prop. 10.7) is immobilized. When power is widely dispersed (Prop. 10.8), compromise issues can be ratified but cannot be decided by the dominant coalition in toto.

In the organization with dispersed power (Prop. 10.9), the central power figure is the individual who can manage the coalition.

11

the administrative process

Modern societies have been busier making complex organizations work, largely through trial and error, than studying them. As a result we have no clear picture of what administration is or what it does, either for organizations or society, and we have no consensus on the nature of the administrative process. Available "principles" of administration or management are essentially statements derived from rational-model assumptions, and tend to be normative rather than always realistic.

Whatever we say about administration, of course, is governed by what phenomena we refer to by the term, and that is an arbitrary matter. The approach taken in this volume, that complex purposive organizations are natural systems subject to rationality norms, permits us to suggest that the significant phenomena of administration arise precisely because of the inconsistencies of that duality. If complex organizations were simply natural systems, we might expect spontaneous processes to handle their problems. If complex organizations were simply rational-model machines, they would require designers to initiate them, but their operation thereafter would be automatic. It is because the organization is not simply either, we suggest, that administration emerges as an identifiable and important process in modern societies.

From this point of view, the available principles of administration derived from rational-model assumptions apply to those portions of organizations which are so protected from exogenous variables that the closed system of logic is practical, but it would be a mistake to assume that such principles equal administration.

While our exploration of organizations in action does not permit us to offer a new set of principles more inclusive than present ones, it does enable us to suggest some of the elements which may have to be incorporated in a new and fuller understanding of administration. For unless we have been far astray, there are important problems for complex organizations which cannot be settled spontaneously and which are not hinted at by prescriptions derived from the rational model.

We have argued, for example, that the organization must find and maintain a viable technology—that it must have some capacity to satisfy demands of a task environment, and that these demands may be changing. In the society geared to complex organizations, technologies change as cause/effect understandings change; hence a technology that was effective yesterday may be inadequate today. Or yesterday's viable technology may be viable again today but with a different set of partners, a new task environment. Questions of which technology to retain, which to expel, and which to adopt may not be daily matters for any complex organization, but they are potential problems for every organization in a modern society, and we see no reason to believe that they get solved spontaneously or via the closed logic of the rational model.

We indeed have empirical reasons for believing that such problems are experienced as knotty ones by those involved in the administrative process. Hitler's use of paratroops against enemy defenses organized for stationary warfare is an historic example, and Billy Mitchell became a martyr while advocating air technology for military purposes. The technology question is currently symbolized in industry by questions of what, and how fast, to automate, but it has parallels in other fields. Hospital administrators, for example, may worry about the merits and demerits of intensive care centers with electronic monitoring of multiple patients, or the introduction of self-service hotel facilities for ambulatory patients. Educational administrators have parallel worries about teaching machines, team-teaching techniques, and possible programs for breaking the intergenerational perpetuation of drop outs.

In these and other fields, solutions are not easily come by, for the adoption of new technologies reduces the value of present resources—whether physical or human—and introduces elements of uncertainty; the alternative of finding a new task environment requires establishing new dependencies and thus new contingencies.

Protection of technical cores from overwhelming uncertainties or contingencies in the environment was also advanced as a central problem for the organization. We have argued that the protection necessary to enable achievement by technical cores may be afforded by domain maneuvering or by modifications in organizational design, but we have no reason to believe that either will happen spontaneously, and there is no closed-system solution to the alternatives posed.

We have asserted that an organization structure must be developed and maintained consistent with technological requirements yet at the same time consistent with input and output requirements and the realities of the task environment. In the small and simple organization this fitting and modification of structure may be autonomous and spontaneous, but in the large and complicated organization, the conversion of uncertainties into certainties becomes something less than obvious (Thompson, 1964), and interdependence radiates. Again, neither spontaneity nor closed-system logic can govern structure.

We have implied that every complex organization has some combination of three types of interdependence, and therefore requires some combination of three basic types of coordination. But there is no spontaneous mechanism which confines the application of rules to those areas where uniformity is needed, or which adjusts rules to the needs for scheduling flexibility or intensive judgment. The proper dovetailing of several forms of coordination is not handled by the natural-system approach, nor is it treated within the rational-model approach.

We have argued that assessment of components and of the whole is of basic importance to organizations subject to achievement norms, and it seems clear that the subtle complications in assessment call for something more than automatic or closed-logic solutions. Assessment seems to be an administrative problem.

Finally, we have maintained that inducements/contributions contracts must be arranged and at times adjusted, in order to elicit the inputs necessary for organizational action. In the small and simple organization, this too may be automatic, but in the large and complicated organization with a heterogeneous and dynamic task environment, this is a never-ending and deliberate matter, an administrative matter.

It is our view that any description of administration which ignores the kinds of problems enumerated above is insufficient. But the enumeration of administrative problems is inevitably misleading, for it casts thought into a one-matter-at-a-time framework, while the essence of administration lies in their configuration.

CO-ALIGNMENT: THE BASIC ADMINISTRATIVE FUNCTION

We and others have emphasized the coalitional nature of complex organizations, but always in terms of agreements among individual members, each having something to contribute and each receiving something in exchange. There is, however, a larger sense of configuration, which we will refer to as *co-alignment*.

Perpetuation of the complex organization rests on an appropriate co-alignment in time and space not simply of human individuals but of streams of institutionalized action. Survival rests on the co-alignment of technology and task environment with a viable domain, and of organization design and structure appropriate to that domain.

The co-alignment we assert to be the basic administrative function is not a simple combination of static components. Each of the elements involved in the co-alignment has its own dynamics. Each behaves at its own rate, governed by forces external to the organization. Technology, for example, is embedded in the cause/effect belief systems of a wider environment. The rate of obsolescence and the direction of innovation in that wider environment may be predictable, but the organization can neither prevent nor command innovation or obsolescence. Personnel resources are similarly governed by institutionalized patterns. Although in modern societies the institutions of job and career, and the associated opportunity structures, result from the aggregate actions of many organizations, seldom can the organization in the short run make more than a ripple in those institutional patterns (Moore and Feldman, 1960). The specific organization must work within that stream of action as it finds it. Similarly, the financial acts of the organization contribute to the aggregate patterns of investment and cash flows, but at any particular time the organization must fit itself into those patterns (Parsons and Smelser, 1956). Boundaries of legitimacy may be influenced by organizations in the aggregate, but for any specific organization at any specific time those boundaries are determined largely by legislative, executive, or judicial developments which have their own history and dynamics.

Clienteles possess demographic characteristics and trends which the individual organization may be able to project and to which it may adapt, but which it can hardly control. Age and sex distributions are subject to biological dynamics; geographic distributions, to economic, political and social forces which are bigger than any organization.

Now if the elements necessary to the co-alignment are in part influenced by powerful forces in the organization's environment, then organization survival requires *adaptive* as well as *directive* action in those areas where the organization maintains discretion. Since each of the necessary streams of institutional action moves at its own rate, the timing of both adaptive and directive action is a crucial administrative matter. As environments change, the administrative process must deal not just with which domain, but how and how fast to change the design, structure, or technology of the organization.

Thus, in our view, the central function of administration is to keep the organization at the *nexus* of several necessary streams of action; and because the several streams are variable and moving, the nexus is not only moving but sometimes quite difficult to fathom.

We must emphasize that organizations are not simply determined by their environments. Administration may innovate on any or all of the necessary dimensions, but only to the extent that the innovations are acceptable to those on whom the organization must and can depend. The organization must conform to the "rules of the game" or somehow negotiate a revised set of rules.

But if the organization is not simply the product of its environment, neither is it independent. The configuration necessary for survival comes neither from yielding to any and all pressures nor from manipulating all variables, but from finding the *strategic variables* (Barnard, 1938)—those which are available to the organization and can be manipulated in such a way that interaction with other elements will result in a viable co-alignment.

The Paradox of Administration

If the basic function of administration involves shooting at a moving target of co-alignment, in which the several components of that target are themselves moving, then we can expect the central characteristic of the administrative process to be a search for flexibility. Yet our theme throughout has been one of reduction of uncertainty and its conversion into relative certainty. How do we meet this apparent paradox?

The administrative hierarchy, often described as "channels," appears to be a dual-purpose mechanism, progressively eliminating or absorbing uncertainty (March and Simon, 1958) as we move from higher to lower levels, and progressively affording flexibility as we move from lower to higher levels. The first purpose has been thoroughly treated in the literature of administration, and perhaps most succinctly described by Simon (1957) as a process by which each hierarchical level establishes the premises on which the next lower level is to base its decisions. The second purpose is relatively neglected in the literature, but it seems clear that if the coalition or its representatives are to be able to "contract" with elements of the task environment (Hawkes, 1961), the technical core and the managerial layers must afford capacity—and deliverable or unfrozen capacity.

From this perspective, administration is not something done by an administrator except in the simple organization, but instead is a process flowing through the actions of various members. Also from this point of view, administration is not something done at one level in the organization, but is a process spanning and linking levels. Finally, from this viewpoint, administration is not a process which simply flows down from one level to the next, but a process related to the interaction of levels and components.

In the complex organizations, then, we cannot understand administrative behavior by studying it at one level. This can best be illustrated in terms of our decision-making scheme (Chapter 10), as applied to the three major levels distinguished by Parsons (Chapter 1). Technical rationality, which we have said is the priority target at the technical core of the organization, calls basically for the computational decision strategy. Technical rationality is a sensible concept only if outcome preferences are crystallized and cause/effect relationships fairly well defined. Neither of these conditions can be satisfied within the technical core of the organization, except as higher levels provide them. We would expect the outcome preferences, or "goals of the organization," to be specified by what Parsons terms the "institutional level" of the organization (and which we would define as composed of the inner circle, as discussed in Chapter 10). But we would expect specification of cause/effect relationships to be provided by the middle or managerial level of the hierarchy. This does not imply that managers are technical inventors, but rather that they control the kinds of resources inputs obtained and the kinds of interdependence that is recognized and reflected in organization structure.

Thus our approach to organizations and administration suggests that the technical level of the administrative hierarchy is dependent on higher levels to provide the conditions necessary to approach technical rationality. But by the same token the other end of the administrative hierarchy is dependent on the technical core and the managerial level to provide the capacities and the slack (March and Simon, 1958) which allow the organization to make demands on its environment and to take advantage of opportunities afforded by that environment.

The paradox of administration, the dual searches for certainty and flexibility, to a large extent revolves around the dimension of time. In the *short run,* administration seeks the reduction or elimination of uncertainty in order to score well on assessments of technical rationality. In the *long run,* however, we would expect administration to strive for flexibility through freedom from commitment—i.e., slack—for the larger the fund of uncommitted capacities, the greater the organization's assurance of self-control in an uncertain future.

Economic debates have made us well aware of the problems of determining, operationally, the difference between long run and short run, and it is this distinction that divides the desire for certainty from the desire for slack. How far into the future the administrative focus goes is a variable to be determined empirically, not by conceptual argument.

Now we are in a position to suggest that the time dimension of concern is inversely related to level in the organization's administrative hierarchy. Thus at the upper reaches, or institutional level, we would expect the short run to be relatively insignificant and the longer run to be of central concern. Here we would expect the focus to be on increasing or maintaining flexibility and command of uncommitted or easily recommittable resources. At the other extreme, the technical core, we would expect concern for certainty in the short run to drive out consideration of the longer run. The central part of the administrative hierarchy, the managerial layer, would thereby become the "translator," securing from the institutional level sufficient commitments to permit technical achievement, yet securing from the technical core sufficient capacity and slack to permit administrative discretion and, if necessary, recommitment of resources.

VARIATIONS IN ADMINISTRATIVE PROCESS

The above discussion of administration is an idealized version, a picture of what administration is or would achieve in the perpetually healthy organization. Obviously some organizations die, and some suffer for considerable periods of time with ailments of one sort or another; the administrative process frequently departs from the ideal. Are these departures random, or can we find patterns?

Administrative Styles

Cyert and March (1963) have introduced the important concept of problemistic search, in connection with organizational decision making. They define problemistic search as search that is stimulated by a problem and directed toward finding a solution to that problem. It is thus distinguished from random curiosity and from the search for understanding per se. In the Cyert and March behavioral theory of the firm—and undoubtedly in much real-life organizational behavior—search is "simple-minded," reflecting simple concepts of causality, and initially is based on two simple rules: (1) search in the neighborhood of the problem symptom and (2) search in the neighborhood of the current alternative. When these two rules do not produce an acceptable solution, they add a third: (3) search in organizationally vulnerable areas; that is, in areas where slack exists or where power is weak.

We can subscribe to these propositions as describing the empirically dominant style with which the administrative process is carried out, and yet we need to suggest that it is but one of at least two styles. It is possible to conceive of monitoring behavior which scans the environment for opportunities—which does not wait to be activated by a problem and which does not therefore stop when a problem solution has been found. We will refer to this as *opportunistic surveillance,* and suggest that it is the organizational counterpart to curiosity in the individual.

We would expect problemistic search to be predominant in complex organizations, and we would especially expect to find it in the technical core, or in the managerial layer most closely associated with the technical core, where behavior is oriented and bound within rather tight constraints, and where assessments tend to be made in terms of efficiency or instrumentality. But we have argued that finding a viable nexus is the heart of administration; and in dynamic environments this is not likely to result from problemistic search. On questions of domain, it would seem that the organization which anticipates institutional trends is in a better position to exercise self-control than the organization which waits until the domain problem arises.

Opportunistic surveillance, if it is to be found, should be associated with the institutional level of the organization, according to our reasoning. Yet in every field—education, medicine, industry, commerce, military, and government—instances are apparent where once-robust organizations decline or pass through crises because they have failed to anticipate institutional changes. What accounts for the relative scarcity of opportunistic surveillance? We have no definite answer to that question, but we can seek clues in two directions: (1) in the attributes of administrators as individuals and (2) in the structure of the situations in which they operate. These may be more easily separated conceptually than in fact.

Limitations on the Administrative Process

Perhaps the most widespread limitation on the administrative process results when participants define administration as *officeholding* rather than an essential ingredient in organizational accomplishment. This is likely when rationality norms are weakly enforced.

The officeholding view of administrative positions may occur in the sheltered organization, the organization which has somehow obtained limitless resources or a monopolistic position, and thereby has achieved an unusual degree of independence. In such situations dissatisfaction with or lack of respect for the organization may be present, but the organization's lack of dependence reduces the ability of task-environment elements to make them felt.

Still another situation giving rise to the officeholding view of administration is the captive organization, where power in the organization is based on factors extraneous to organizational achievement. Where family ties, patronage, bribery, or tradition is the basis for participation in the coalition, we would expect intrigue rather than achievement to dominate in administrative circles.

Both of these conditions may be found in the modern society, but they are especially likely in the society not yet geared to complex organizations. In traditional societies, moreover, existing organizations and institutional patterns are assumed to be inevitable. It therefore appears that the individual's efforts may make a difference in his relationship to the organization, but cannot make a difference in the organization itself. This is a basic source of frustration for administrators who have been schooled in modern societies but hold administrative responsibilities in traditional societies.

A second and also widespread limitation on administration seems to be a bias toward certainty, which shows up in various forms including preference for short-term rather than long-term considerations, quantitative rather than qualitative data, and precedent rather than innovation.

At least one personality variable, intolerance for ambiguity (Frenkel-

Brunswik, 1949), seems to be associated with the administrative bias toward certainty. We would expect the individual who is uncomfortable with ambiguity but placed in a situation where action has future consequences, to be oriented to the short run. The consequences of causal action become less predictable as the time horizon extends, for consequences ramify into the future. Precedent, and the assumption that the future will be similar to the past, should also be attractive to the administrator with low tolerance for ambiguity. We indicated in Chapter 9 that individuals uncomfortable with discretion might nevertheless be motivated to occupy positions where discretion resides, and under such conditions, we would expect a bias toward certainty in the administrative process.

Quite apart from the personality variable, however, we might expect the bias toward certainty to occur by default, through weakness in or absence of a definable institutional layer in the organization. If the powerful inner circle (Chapter 10) is composed solely of individuals with responsibilities in the managerial layer, we would expect problemistic search, not opportunistic surveillance, to prevail. The same result can be obtained when nonmanagerial members of the inner circle are personally intolerant of ambiguity. Default at the institutional level, however, is more likely to come because of lack of a sharp distinction, conceptually, between managerial and institutional matters. As Parsons (1960) has suggested, this functional differentiation is clouded by a tradition of a uniform chain of command which makes each successive rank different only in degree from the preceding one. The conversion of administrators from managerial to institutional responsibilities is more than a promotion, for it entails a shift in attention from technical to organizational rationality (Chapter 2), from instrumental to social assessments (Chapter 7).

This structural bias toward certainty is especially likely when elements of the task environment lack sufficient power to challenge the assumptions on which the inner circle bases its actions. Ultimately, of course, task-environment elements do have or achieve such power, but it may be exercised only in the case of bankruptcy, economic or otherwise.

A third major limitation on the administrative process lies in the diffusion of power to the point where no inner circle emerges with sufficient stability to give direction to the organization. Although this situation is more visible at the level of national governments in various parts of the world, we believe it is approached in universities, voluntary hospitals, and local governments with some frequency. Where the power base is widely diffuse and shifting we expect administrative behavior to be problem oriented, not aggressive, and to be safety oriented, not innovative.

A final limitation on the administrative process is lack of knowledge or know-how. As was made clear by Chandler's (1962) study of the development of the modern corporation in the United States, some of the spectacularly successful innovations in organization design and structure came after many years of painful trial and error. The resulting rationality is clear in hindsight, but innovative solutions to basic administrative problems are not easily found.

SOCIAL ASPECTS OF ADMINISTRATION

Societies geared to complex organizations, as we indicated in Chapter 1, lodge heavy proportions of their resources in complex organizations and thereby become dependent on such organizations. Performance errors or failures can have profound consequences for the health or safety of individuals or groups in the task environment of an organization (Boulding, 1953), and failure of an organization to survive may have serious ramifications for careers of many individuals; indeed, for the careers of communities (Cottrell, 1955 and 1951).

Modern societies thus have a stake in the welfare of complex organizations. Societies geared to complex organizations do not depend solely on the sagacity of an inner circle or on the private motives of a large coalition to ensure the survival of complex organizations. True, the modern society may permit or encourage the launching of many small organizations, knowing that they will have high mortality rates, but once an organization has become established and has demonstrated capacities, the social costs of dismantling are large, and dismantling is seldom permitted.

The commuter service, for example, may be unable to establish a domain or to defend one against superhighway competition; yet elements of the environment are reluctant to see the commuter service die, and the result is an enlarged task environment including governmental units to lend support. Business organizations in trouble frequently find it possible to go through bankruptcy, in which the task environment shares in the misfortune, to regain viability. Hospitals, schools, or universities may lose their viability and their identity, but usually not through dismantlement. Rather they are amalgamated into larger organizations.

Such solutions to troubles in organizations are often costly, however, precisely because organizations are significant instruments of modern societies. Their underuse or abuse can have wide consequences. If our thesis in this volume is correct, task environments generally act as constant tests of complex organizations, signaling errors of omission or commission, and often intervening when organizations fail to heed such signals. Yet we know of business bankruptcies which have surprised even the closest associates of the troubled organization, and governmental laxities which remain unnoticed or unspoken until a major scandal erupts. Task-environment policing is not foolproof.

The secondary defense, expansion of the task environment to influence troubled organizations, is an essential social response to the fact of increased social dependence on complex organizations. We see it in hospitals with the rise of third-party payers, who in addition to channeling insurance payments may begin to question performance standards, charges, or the quality of patient care. We see it in public education with the emergence of powerful state and national programs which can set standards and limits on formerly autonomous local boards of education. We see it in business, first with the emergence of centralized associations of firms in an industry, and also with the rise of centralized labor organizations, both with power to intervene in local activities when larger interests are challenged. A somewhat later development (in the western world) has been a tendency for government to be an active member of the task environment for complex organizations of all types, including business and industry.

The Current Challenge to Administration

Reliance on existing or expanded task environments to salvage troubled organizations is costly. By the time these mechanisms work, the organization may be in an advanced stage of abuse, requiring years to overcome. Preventive care, in this case viable administration, is a much less costly way of keeping organizations socially useful.

Undoubtedly the administrative process works brilliantly in some of our most significant organizations as well as in some of the less significant ones. But there is no guarantee that the society which assigns such importance to complex organizations will be able to provide them with administrators equal to the task. Undoubtedly some administrators have deep insight into the nature and workings of organizations and the administrative process, but the conversion of private insight into sharable—teachable and learnable—understanding is not an automatic process.

Systematic understanding of organizations and administration is scarce. Little is known about the preparation of individuals for administrative careers; and technical supervision or management is frequently equated with administration, thus ignoring the crucial institutional role in the process (Selznick, 1957). In American public education, hospitals, and social welfare organizations, the tendency has been to insist that competence related to the organization's technical core be an essential ingredient for the administrator; for example, in most cases, school administrators must hold teaching certificates. We have little systematic evidence of the impact of such practices on administration, but it seems likely that they (1) restrict the scope of an organization's search for administrative abilities and (2) intensify differences between professionals and lay boards in the administrative process (Thompson, 1962a).

We know that the sources of administrators, and the career preparation or experience they may receive, can differ from society to society (Harbison and Myers, 1959), but we know very little about the consequences of such differences for the administrative process. The societal dependence on complex organizations has led to the establishment of professional schools or departments for the training of administrators— business, public, medical, educational, social work, etc.—in American universities and in various kinds of institutes in many parts of Europe and Asia. Yet even in America, which pioneered in modern education for administration, such schools are still trying to rise out of the stage of relaying current practices and exhorting "good works." The research base which might enable such schools to mold future practice is conspicuously short.

The conclusion seems inescapable that the society which depends mightily on complex organizations is going to have to give serious attention to the administration of such organizations.

The Frontier of Administration

Civilization seems inescapably to bring with it the expansion of interdependencies. Complex organizations appear to be social responses to enlarged networks of cause/effect relationships, and we have suggested (Prop. 4.1) that organizations will grow in the direction of their most crucial dependencies. But the gearing of society to complex organizations, together with the institutionalization of scientific research and the resulting expansion of interdependencies, seems to be creating needs for action on a scope even larger than the capacity of our organizations.

Bluntly speaking, social purposes in modern societies increasingly exceed the capacities of complex organizations, and call instead for action by multiorganization complexes. This may be seen, for example, in the custom construction of giant hydroelectric dams, which call for the combined efforts of several giant construction organizations. It may be seen in space exploration, which calls for the research, developmental, engineering, and production efforts of a complex of organizations, organized around a "prime contractor." It may be seen in the multistate port authority, in the combine of universities to operate jointly a costly and scarce research facility. It appears in highly complicated form in the movement to improve the teaching of physical sciences in the secondary schools of the United States, as described by Clark (1965). The movement was spearheaded by Professor Zacharias as head of a committee of university professors and secondary school teachers. This group of professional scientists and educators was joined by the National Science Foundation, an arm of the Federal government, which financed the committee's work. The resulting teaching materials were made available to the nation's school systems by being distributed through normal commercial channels. The National Science Foundation supported a program of summer institutes offered by colleges to train teachers in the use of the new materials. Within ten years from the initiation of the project, more than forty per cent of high school students studying physics were studying the new materials, in spite of the fact that adoption of the materials remains officially a matter for local school board decision.

What emerges from Clark's analysis is a marshaling of resources from diverse sources in an effective sequence to bring about a result that was beyond the ability of any single organization. A Federal agency provided the initial funds, a private nonprofit group developed a new course, commercial organizations made the new materials available throughout the decentralized educational system, varied universities and colleges trained teachers to use the new materials, and local authorities adopted the new materials and permitted teachers to revise local courses.

RECAPITULATION

The basic function of administration appears to be co-alignment, not merely of people (in coalitions) but of institutionalized action—of technology and task environment into a viable domain, and of organizational design and structure appropriate to it. Administration, when it works well, keeps the organization at the nexus of the several necessary streams of action. Paradoxically, the administrative process must reduce uncertainty but at the same time search for flexibility.

Administrative decision making frequently rests on problemistic search, expecially in and around the technical core, but opportunistic surveillance is also needed, especially at the institutional level. It may fail to materialize if rationality norms are weak, if administrators are biased toward certainty, or if power is too diffuse to be mobilized to give stability and direction to the organization.

The administrative process may also be limited by sheer lack of knowledge and insight into new situations. The achievement of high levels of technical rationality has indeed been a major accomplishment of modern societies, and similar accomplishments by societies now in transition present important challenges. But in modern societies, it appears, we have passed from the era in which control and coordination of technological activities were the central administrative challenge, into an era in which organizational rationality is the core of administration, and the administration of multiorganization projects and activities is the central challenge. Whether we have or will gain the knowledge about the organizations that it takes to use and control them under conditions of extreme interdependence remains to be seen.

conclusion

Organizations in Action: Universal Aspects

Uncertainty appears as the fundamental problem for complex organizations, and coping with uncertainty, as the essence of the administrative process.

Just as complete uncertainty or randomness is the antithesis of purpose and of organization, complete certainty is a figment of the imagination; but the tighter the norms of rationality, the more energy the organization will devote to moving toward certainty.

Uncertainties are presented to complex organizations from three sources, two external to the organization and the third internal. External uncertainties stem from (1) *generalized uncertainty,* or lack of cause/effect understanding in the culture at large, and (2) *contingency,* in which the outcomes of organizational action are in part determined by the actions of elements of the environment. The internal source of uncertainty is (3) *interdependence of components.* Solution of the first type provides a pattern against which organizational action can be ordered.

Solution of the second type affords organizational freedom to so order action against the pattern. Solution of the third results in the actual ordering of action to fit the pattern.

Whatever the private motives of individual members, they must be translated into an organizational domain or set of responsibilities which members and others can recognize as organizational purpose. Having one or more purposes, the organization's first and worst problem is generalized uncertainty. Purpose without cause/effect understanding provides no basis for recognizing alternatives, no grounds for claiming credit for success or escaping blame for failure, no pattern for self-control. Where purpose is present but patterns are vague, organizational survival becomes not simply an underlying necessity but a conscious and pressing goal of those in the organization's power structure. Extrinsic evaluations are emphasized, together with ceremonial reaffirmations of the importance or sacredness of the purpose. The search for more effective procedures is characteristic, and technological fads are prevalent.

When purpose and cause/effect understanding are present, the basic threat to organizational success lies in interdependence with an environment which may be uncooperative. Under these conditions, organizations try to achieve predictability and self-control through regulation of transactions at their boundaries—through negotiation, by buffering, or by varying their own activities to match fluctuations in the environment. The location of discretionary positions and the number and nature of the structural units at the boundaries of the organization are determined by the need to regulate boundary transactions. If these cannot be regulated satisfactorily, the organization tries to move its boundaries—to incorporate or encircle unreliable units.

To the extent that boundaries are regulated, cause/effect relationships are known, and purpose is present; internal interdependence is the potential source of uncertainty. Now the organization seeks self-control through coordination of the actions of its components, through subordinating each component to a monolithic authority network with centralized decision making.

Although frequently cited as symbolic of complex organizations, the monolithic authority network with centralized decision making is not typical of complex organizations in modern societies, for it is appropriate only when closed-system conditions are approximated. Where boundary contingencies or internal interdependencies are numerous, organizations need bounded rationality for local handling of those uncertainties. Where both internal processes and boundary transactions are highly variable, the bounding of rationality requires structural decentralization, the creation of semiautonomous subsystems.

The kinds of actions described above may be at odds with certain ideologies or traditions, and hence may be taken only reluctantly or in desperation; but we believe they represent necessary adaptations to technological and task-environmental uncertainties and therefore that they emerge when rationality norms are seriously enforced. We believe they are universal tendencies.

Organizations in Action: Variable Aspects

The fact that we expect all organizations to seek the same state—self-control—does not mean that we expect all of them to attain it in the same way, with identical design, structures, or behavior. It is essential that we find universals, but equally essential to find patterns in variations.

At various points, therefore, we have asserted that the design, structure, or behavior of organizations will vary systematically with differences in technologies. If our understanding of organizations is to grow, we must compare organizations with different technologies; but to do so we must learn to categorize technologies with some precision. The old categories of business, medical, educational, or governmental organizations simply are inadequate for the development of theory.

In a variety of ways we have also asserted that the design, structure, and behavior of organizations will reflect variations in task environments; and if that is true we must learn to make systematic comparisons of organizations in terms of their task environments. To do so we must do more than merely compare organizations by industry; by local, state, or national scope; or by cultural contexts. For leverage on this problem, new conceptual developments are essential.

Whatever the ultimate conceptualization of task environments, it seems clear that we need to take explicit notice of and systematically compare the institutionalized patterns which are incorporated in cultures and societies. Organizations may, on occasion, take these for granted and get away with it; but such institutionalized patterns as contract, career, or credit are important factors in organizational action and cannot be taken for granted in a theory of organizational action. We also need to investigate how norms of rationality emerge in modern societies, how they may vary, and the conditions under which they are applied and enforced.

The Administrative Process

The process of administration may be thought of as providing boundaries within which organizational rationality becomes possible. In this view administration is a process of coping with uncertainty, but it is not merely the defensive absorption or blockage of uncertainty. Administration includes a more aggressive co-alignment aspect which keeps the organization at a nexus of several necessary streams of action. Bounded rationality involves not only the reduction of complexity by the elimination of uncertainty or provision of certainty equivalents, but also the incorporation within the arena for action of the variables necessary for purposive action.

Administration arises from the need for discretion to handle open-system problems of generalized and contingent uncertainty. The ability to provide such discretion is the basis for power in the administrative process.

We must conclude that there is no one best way, no single evolutionary continuum through which organizations pass; hence, no single set of activities which constitute administration. Appropriateness of design, structure, and assessments can be judged only in light of the conditions, variables, and uncertainties present for the organization; and these judgments are bound to be significantly influenced by the perceptions and beliefs of those participating in the administrative process.

The relative importance of different uncertainties and the relative costs of offsetting or eliminating or avoiding them are matters to be estimated—by variable human agents. The ways in which uncertainties are perceived, the responses which are considered appropriate to those uncertainties, and the resulting rapidity of adaptation to the realities of technology and task environment are determined by the variability of the humans involved in the administrative process. Here again we need comparative analysis.

Organizations and Societies

Complex organizations exist ultimately as agencies of their environments, acquiring resources in exchange for outputs and, in the final analysis, obtaining technologies from environments. But task environments never are as extensive as societies, and there can be pockets in which several organizations operate in mutual support in a network which is itself at odds with the larger society. The fact that organizations exist with the consent of their environments does not automatically subject them to societal control.

We have no assurance that modern societies have yet developed procedures for assessing the value of the kinds of organizations modern societies are developing, but because these are powerful instruments we can expect modern societies to exhibit considerable concern over the uses and abuses of complex organizations.

Modern societies must also struggle with questions of developing and allocating human capacities for the administration of complex organizations. Comparative analyses of the sources, capacities, and behavior of administrators in various societies are essential if we are to understand organizations in action, or control them.

Research Directions

Unless questions are asked about technologies and task environments, concepts adequate for the analysis of these dimensions are not likely to be developed or refined. But without refinement of the rather crude concepts we have been using, we are not going to get very far in testing hypotheses or in asking more sophisticated questions. Both theoretical development and empirical investigation hinge on the adequacy of concepts.

The propositions offered in this volume have been stated in the form which allows them to be negated if incorrect; when certain empirical conditions are found, we say, certain other empirical things will also be found. Testable form is not enough, however. We must have operations which will enable us to say that in fact the specified conditions do or do not exist. Here again, operationalization must proceed hand in hand with conceptual refinement.

Hopefully our propositions seem plausible and important, but it is unlikely that many will be treated as hypotheses for extensive testing, for in the process of the necessary conceptual refinement, more specific and subtle hypotheses will be generated. Our hope and intention has not been to state eternal truths but to focus theoretical and empirical attention on organizational action by stating as forcefully as possible the need to study organizations in toto and, for that purpose, the significance of the open-system approach and the certainty/uncertainty dimension.

bibliography

Abegglen, James C.: *The Japanese Factory*, New York: The Free Press of Glencoe, 1958.

Anderson, Theodore R., and Seymour Warkov: "Organizational Size and Functional Complexity: A Study of Administration in Hospitals," *American Sociological Review*, vol. 26, February, 1961, pp. 23–28.

Argyris, Chris: *Executive Leadership*, New York: Harper & Row, Publishers, Incorporated, 1953.

———: *Organization of a Bank*, New Haven, Conn.: Labor and Management Center, Yale University, 1954.

Ashby, W. Ross: *An Introduction to Cybernetics*, London: Chapman and Hall, Ltd., 1956.

Atkinson, John W.: "Motivational Determinants of Risk-taking Behavior," *Psychological Review*, vol. 64, November, 1957, pp. 359–372.

Barnard, Chester I.: *The Functions of the Executive*, Cambridge, Mass.: Harvard University Press, 1938.

Bartlett, Sir Frederic: *Thinking: An Experimental and Social Study,* New York: Basic Books, Inc., Publishers, 1958.

Baumol, W. J.: *Business Behavior, Value and Growth,* New York: The Macmillan Company, 1959.

Becker, Howard S., and Anselm L. Strauss: "Careers, Personality, and Adult Socialization," *American Journal of Sociology,* vol. 62, November, 1956, pp. 253–263.

Belknap, Ivan: *The Human Problems of a State Mental Hospital,* New York: McGraw-Hill Book Company, 1956.

Berelson, Bernard, and Gary A. Steiner: *Human Behavior: An Inventory of Scientific Findings,* New York: Harcourt, Brace and World, Inc., 1964.

Berliner, Joseph S.: *Factory and Manager in the USSR,* Cambridge, Mass.: Harvard University Press, 1957.

Bidwell, Charles E.: "The School as a Formal Organization," in James G. March (ed.), *Handbook of Organizations,* Chicago: Rand McNally & Company, 1965.

—— and Rebecca S. Vreeland: "College Education and Moral Orientations: An Organizational Approach," *Administrative Science Quarterly,* vol. 8, September, 1963, pp. 166–191.

Blau, Peter M.: *The Dynamics of Bureaucracy,* Chicago: The University of Chicago Press, 1955.

——: *Exchange and Power in Social Life,* New York: John Wiley & Sons, Inc., 1964.

Boulding, Kenneth E.: "A Pure Theory of Conflict Applied to Organizations," in George Fisk (ed.), *The Frontiers of Management Psychology,* New York: Harper & Row, Publishers, Incorporated, 1964.

——: *The Organizational Revolution,* New York: Harper & Row, Publishers, Incorporated, 1953.

Callahan, Raymond E.: *Education and the Cult of Efficiency,* Chicago: The University of Chicago Press, 1962.

Caplow, Theodore: *Principles of Organization,* New York: Harcourt, Brace and World, Inc., 1964.

—— and Reece J. McGee: *The Academic Marketplace,* New York: Basic Books, Inc., Publishers, 1958.

Carlson, Richard O.: "Environmental Constraints and Organizational Consequences: The Public School and Its Clients," in *Behavioral*

Science and Educational Administration, 1964, Chicago: National Society for the Study of Education, 1964.

———: *Executive Succession and Organizational Change,* Chicago: Mid-West Administration Center, University of Chicago, 1962.

Carlson, Sune: *Executive Behavior,* Stockholm: Strömberg Aktiebolag, 1951.

Chandler, Alfred D., Jr.: *Strategy and Structure,* Cambridge, Mass.: The M.I.T. Press, 1962.

Clark, Burton R.: *Adult Education in Transition,* Berkeley, Calif.: University of California Press, 1956.

———: "Interorganizational Patterns in Education," *Administrative Science Quarterly,* vol. 10, September, 1965, pp. 224–237.

Cloward, Richard A.: "Social Control in the Prison," in Richard A. Cloward et al., *Social Control in the Prison,* New York: Social Science Research Council, 1960.

Cohen, Albert K.: "The Sociology of the Deviant Act: Anomie Theory and Beyond," *American Sociological Review,* vol. 30, February, 1965, pp. 5–13.

Coleman, James S.: *Community Conflict,* New York: The Free Press of Glencoe, 1957.

Cooper, William W., Harold J. Leavitt, and Maynard W. Shelly II (eds.): *New Perspectives in Organization Research,* New York: John Wiley & Sons, Inc., 1964.

Costello, Timothy W., Joseph F. Kubis, and Charles L. Shaffer: "An Analysis of Attitudes Toward a Planned Merger," *Administrative Science Quarterly,* vol. 8, September, 1963, pp. 235–250.

Cottrell, W. Fred: "Death by Dieselization: A Case Study in the Reaction to Technological Change," *American Sociological Review,* vol. 16, June, 1951, pp. 358–365.

———: *Energy and Society,* New York: McGraw-Hill Book Company, 1955.

Cressy, Donald R.: "Prison Organizations," in James G. March (ed.), *Handbook of Organizations,* Chicago: Rand McNally & Company, 1965.

Crozier, Michel: *The Bureaucratic Phenomenon,* Chicago: The University of Chicago Press, 1964.

Cyert, Richard M., W. R. Dill, and James G. March: "The Role of Expectations in Business Decision Making," *Administrative Science Quarterly,* vol. 3, December, 1958, pp. 307–340.

—— and James G. March: *A Behavioral Theory of the Firm,* Englewood Cliffs, N.J.: Prentice-Hall, Inc., 1963.

Dale, Ernest: *The Great Organizers,* New York: McGraw-Hill Book Company, 1960.

Dalton, Melville: *Men Who Manage,* New York: John Wiley & Sons, Inc., 1959.

Dill, William R.: "Desegregation or Integration? Comments about Contemporary Research on Organizations," in W. W. Cooper, Harold J. Leavitt, and Maynard W. Shelly II (eds.), *New Perspectives in Organization Research,* New York: John Wiley & Sons, Inc., 1964.

——: "Environment as an Influence on Managerial Autonomy," *Administrative Science Quarterly,* vol. 2, March, 1958, pp. 409–443.

——, Thomas L. Hilton, and Walter R. Reitman: *The New Managers,* Englewood Cliffs, N.J.: Prentice-Hall, Inc., 1962.

Dinerman, Helen: "Image Problems for American Companies Abroad," in John W. Riley, Jr. (ed.), *The Corporation and Its Publics,* New York: John Wiley & Sons, Inc., 1963.

Dornbusch, Sanford M.: "The Military Academy as an Assimilating Institution," *Social Forces,* vol. 33, May, 1955, pp. 316–321.

Dubin, Robert: "Stability of Human Organizations," in Mason Haire (ed.), *Modern Organization Theory,* New York: John Wiley & Sons, Inc., 1959.

Eaton, Joseph W.: "Symbolic and Substantive Evaluative Research," *Administrative Science Quarterly,* vol. 6, March, 1962, pp. 421–442.

Elling, Ray H., and Sandor Halebsky: "Organizational Differentiation and Support: A Conceptual Framework," *Administrative Science Quarterly,* vol. 6, September, 1961, pp. 185–209.

Emerson, Richard M.: "Power-Dependence Relations," *American Sociological Review,* vol. 27, February, 1962, pp. 31–40.

Evan, William M.: "The Organization-Set: Toward a Theory of Interorganizational Relations," in James D. Thompson (ed.), *Approaches to Organizational Design,* Pittsburgh, Pa.: The University of Pittsburgh Press, 1966.

Festinger, Leon: "Informal Social Communication," *Psychological Review*, vol. 57, September, 1950, pp. 271–292.

Fox, Renée C.: "Training for Uncertainty," in Robert K. Merton, George G. Reader, and Patricia L. Kendall (eds.), *The Student-Physician*, Cambridge, Mass.: Harvard University Press, 1957.

Francis, Roy G., and Robert C. Stone: *Service and Procedure in Bureaucracy*, Minneapolis: The University of Minnesota Press, 1956.

Frank, Andrew G.: "Goal Ambiguity and Conflicting Standards," *Human Organization*, vol. 17, Spring, 1958, pp. 8–13.

Frenkel-Brunswik, Else: "Intolerance of Ambiguity as an Emotional and Perceptual Personality Variable," *Journal of Personality*, vol. 18, September, 1949, pp. 108–143.

Galbraith, John K.: *American Capitalism: The Concept of Countervailing Power*, Boston: Houghton Mifflin Company, 1958.

Goffman, Erving: "The Characteristics of Total Institutions," in Walter Reed Institute of Research, *Symposium on Preventive and Social Psychiatry*, Washington, D.C.: U.S. Government Printing Office, 1957.

Goldner, Fred: "Demotion in Industrial Management," *American Sociological Review*, vol. 30, October, 1965, pp. 714–724.

Gore, William J.: *Administrative Decision-making*, New York: John Wiley & Sons, Inc., 1964.

————: "Administrative Decision-Making in Federal Field Offices," *Public Administration Review*, vol. 16, Autumn, 1956, pp. 281–291.

Gouldner, Alvin W.: "Cosmopolitans and Locals: Toward an Analysis of Latent Social Roles," *Administrative Science Quarterly*, vol. 2, December, 1957, and March, 1958, pp. 281–306, 444–480.

————: "Organizational Analysis," in Robert K. Merton, Leonard Broom, and Leonard S. Cottrell, Jr. (eds.), *Sociology Today*, New York: Basic Books, Inc., Publishers, 1959.

————: *Patterns of Industrial Bureaucracy*, New York: The Free Press of Glencoe, 1954.

Granick, David: *Management of the Industrial Firm in the USSR*, New York: Columbia University Press, 1959.

Grusky, Oscar: "Managerial Succession and Organizational Effectiveness," *American Journal of Sociology*, vol. 69, July, 1963, pp. 21–31.

————: "Role Conflict in Organization: A Study of Prison Camp Officials," *Administrative Science Quarterly,* vol. 3, March, 1959, pp. 452–472.

Guest, Robert H.: *Organizational Change: The Effect of Successful Leadership,* Homewood, Ill.: Dorsey Press, 1962.

Gulick, Luther, and L. Urwick (eds.): *Papers on the Science of Administration,* New York: Institute of Public Administration, 1937.

Gusfield, Joseph R.: "Social Structure and Moral Reform: A Study of the Woman's Christian Temperance Union," *American Journal of Sociology,* vol. 61, November, 1955, pp. 221–232.

Haire, Mason: "Biological Models and Empirical Histories of the Growth of Organizations," in Mason Haire (ed.), *Modern Organization Theory,* New York: John Wiley & Sons, Inc., 1959.

————: "Size, Shape and Function in Industrial Organizations," *Human Organization,* vol. 14, Spring, 1955, pp. 17–22.

Hall, Edward T.: *The Silent Language,* Garden City, N.Y.: Doubleday & Company, Inc., 1959.

Harbison, Frederick H., Ernst Köchling, Frank H. Cassell, and Heinrich C. Ruebmann: "Steel Management on Two Continents," *Management Science,* vol. 2, October, 1955, pp. 31–39.

———— and Charles A. Myers: *Management in the Industrial World: An International Analysis,* New York: McGraw-Hill Book Company, 1959.

Hartmann, Heinz: *Authority and Organization in German Management.* Princeton, N.J.: Princeton University Press, 1959.

Hawkes, Robert W.: "Physical Psychiatric Rehabilitation Models Compared," paper presented to the Ohio Valley Sociological Society, 1962.

————: "The Role of the Psychiatric Administrator," *Administrative Science Quarterly,* vol. 6, June, 1961, pp. 89–106.

Hawley, Amos H., Walter Boland, and Margaret Boland: "Population Size and Administration in Institutions of Higher Education," *American Sociological Review,* vol. 30, April, 1965, pp. 252–255.

Homans, George C.: *Social Behavior: Its Elementary Forms,* New York: Harcourt, Brace and World, Inc., 1961.

————: "Social Behavior as Exchange," *American Journal of Sociology,* vol. 63, May, 1958, pp. 597–608.

Howton, F. William: "Work Assignment and Interpersonal Relations," *Administrative Science Quarterly*, vol. 7, March, 1963, pp. 502–520.

Hughes, Everett C.: *Men and Their Work*, New York: The Free Press of Glencoe, 1958.

Hyman, Herbert H.: "The Psychology of Status," *Archives of Psychology*, no. 269, 1942.

Janowitz, Morris: "Changing Patterns of Organizational Authority: The Military Establishment," *Administrative Science Quarterly*, vol. 3, March, 1959, pp. 473–493.

Jaques, Elliott: *The Measurement of Responsibility*, Cambridge, Mass.: Harvard University Press, 1956.

Jones, Kathleen, and Roy Sidebotham: *Mental Hospitals at Work*, London: Routledge & Kegan Paul, Ltd., 1962.

Jones, Maxwell: *The Therapeutic Community*, New York: Basic Books, Inc., Publishers, 1953.

Knauth, Oswald W.: *Business Practices, Trade Position, and Competition*, New York: Columbia University Press, 1956.

Kriesberg, Louis: "Occupational Controls Among Steel Distributors," *American Journal of Sociology*, vol. 61, November, 1955, pp. 203–212.

Landes, David S.: "French Business and the Businessman: A Social and Cultural Analysis," in Edward Mead Earle (ed.), *Modern France*, Princeton, N.J.: Princeton University Press, 1951.

Lee, Dorothy: "Lineal and Nonlineal Codifications of Reality," *Psychometric Medicine*, vol. 12, March-April, 1950, pp. 89–97.

Lentz, Edith M.: "Hospital Administration—One of a Species," *Administrative Science Quarterly*, vol. 1, March, 1957, pp. 444–463.

Levine, Sol, and Paul E. White: "Exchange as a Conceptual Framework for the Study of Interorganizational Relationships," *Administrative Science Quarterly*, vol. 5, March, 1961, pp. 583–601.

Lewin, Kurt: *A Dynamic Theory of Personality*, New York: McGraw-Hill Book Company, 1935.

Litwak, Eugene: "Models of Bureaucracy Which Permit Conflict," *American Journal of Sociology*, vol. 67, September, 1961, pp. 177–184.

—— and Lydia F. Hylton: "Inter-Organizational Analysis," *Administrative Science Quarterly*, vol. 6, March, 1962, pp. 395–420.

Luce, R. Duncan, and Howard Raiffa: *Games and Decisions*, New York: John Wiley & Sons, Inc., 1957.

McClelland, David G.: *The Achieving Society*, Princeton, N.J.: D. Van Nostrand, Inc., 1961.

———, J. W. Atkinson, R. A. Clark, and E. L. Lowell: *The Achievement Motive*, New York: Appleton-Century-Crofts, Inc., 1953.

Macaulay, Stewart: "Non-Contractual Relations in Business: A Preliminary Study," *American Sociological Review*, vol. 28, February, 1963, pp. 55–67.

March, James G.: "The Business Firm as a Political Coalition," *The Journal of Politics*, vol. 24, November, 1962, pp. 662–678.

———: "Introduction" in James G. March (ed.), *Handbook of Organizations*, Chicago: Rand McNally & Company, 1965.

——— and Herbert A. Simon: *Organizations*, New York: John Wiley & Sons, Inc., 1958.

Marcson, Simon: *The Scientist in American Industry*, New York: Harper & Row, Publishers, Incorporated, 1960.

Margolis, J.: "The Analysis of the Firm: Rationalism, Conventionalism, and Behavioralism," *Journal of Business*, vol. 31, July, 1958, pp. 187–199.

Mechanic, David: "Sources of Power of Lower Participants in Complex Organizations," *Administrative Science Quarterly*, vol. 7, December, 1962, pp. 349–364.

Meier, Richard L.: "Communications Overload," *Administrative Science Quarterly*, vol. 7, March, 1963, pp. 521–544.

Merton, Robert K.: "Bureaucratic Structure and Personality," in Robert K. Merton (ed.), *Social Theory and Social Structure* (rev. ed.), New York: The Free Press of Glencoe, 1957a.

———: "The Role-set: Problems in Sociological Theory," *British Journal of Sociology*, vol. 8, June, 1957b, pp. 106–120.

———: "Social Structure and Anomie," in Robert K. Merton, *Social Theory and Social Structure* (rev. ed.), New York: The Free Press of Glencoe, 1957c.

———: "The Unanticipated Consequences of Purposive Social Action," *American Sociological Review*, vol. 1, December, 1936, pp. 894–904.

Messinger, Sheldon L.: "Organizational Transformation: A Case Study of a Declining Social Movement," *American Sociological Review*, vol. 20, February, 1955, pp. 3–10.

Miller, Eric J.: "Technology, Territory and Time: The Internal Differentiation of Complex Production Systems," *Human Relations,* vol. 12, August, 1959, pp. 243–272.

Miller, Walter B.: "Two Concepts of Authority," *American Anthropologist,* vol. 57, April, 1955, pp. 271–289.

Moore, Wilbert E., and Arnold S. Feldman: *Labor Commitment and Social Change in Developing Areas,* New York: Social Science Research Council, 1960.

Palamountain, Joseph C., Jr.: *The Politics of Distribution,* Cambridge, Mass.: Harvard University Press, 1955.

Parsons, Talcott: *Structure and Process in Modern Societies,* New York: The Free Press of Glencoe, 1960.

————: *The Structure of Social Action,* New York: McGraw-Hill Book Company, 1937.

———— and Edward A. Shils (eds.): *Toward a General Theory of Action,* Cambridge, Mass.: Harvard University Press, 1951.

———— and Neil J. Smelser: *Economy and Society,* New York: The Free Press of Glencoe, 1956.

Penrose, Edith Tilton: *The Theory of the Growth of the Firm,* New York: John Wiley & Sons, Inc., 1959.

Perrow, Charles: "The Analysis of Goals in Complex Organizations." *American Sociological Review,* vol. 26, December, 1961a, pp. 854–866.

————: "Hospitals: Technology, Structure, and Goals," in James G. March (ed.), *Handbook of Organizations,* Chicago: Rand McNally & Company, 1965.

————: "Organizational Prestige: Some Functions and Dysfunctions," *American Journal of Sociology,* vol. 66, January, 1961b, pp. 335–341.

Redfield, Robert: "The Folk Society," *American Journal of Sociology,* vol. 52, November, 1947, pp. 293–308.

Richman, Barry M.: "Managerial Motivation in Soviet and Czechoslovak Industries: A Comparison," *Academy of Management Journal,* vol. 6, June, 1963, pp. 107–128.

Richardson, Stephen A.: "Organizational Contrasts on British and American Ships," *Administrative Science Quarterly,* vol. 1, September, 1956, pp. 189–207.

Riggs, Fred W.: *Administration in Developing Countries,* Boston: Houghton Mifflin Company, 1964.

Roethlisberger, Fritz J., and W. J. Dickson: *Management and the Worker,* Cambridge, Mass.: Harvard University Press, 1939.

Rosengren, William R.: "Communication, Organization and Conduct in the 'Therapeutic Milieu,'" *Administrative Science Quarterly,* vol. 9, June, 1964, pp. 70–90.

Scheff, Thomas J.: "Decision Rules, Types of Error, and Their Consequences in Medical Diagnosis," *Behavioral Science,* vol. 8, April, 1963, pp. 97–107.

Selznick, Philip: "Foundations of the Theory of Organization," *American Sociological Review,* vol. 13, February, 1948, pp. 25–35.

————: *Leadership in Administration,* Evanston, Ill.: Row, Peterson, 1957.

————: *TVA and the Grass Roots,* Berkeley, Calif.: University of California Press, 1949.

Shultz, George P., and Thomas L. Whisler (eds.): *Management Organization and the Computer,* New York: The Free Press of Glencoe, 1960.

Siegel, Sidney, and Lawrence E. Fouraker: *Bargaining and Group Decision Making: Experiments in Bilateral Monopoly,* New York: McGraw-Hill Book Company, 1960.

Sills, David L.: *The Volunteers,* New York: The Free Press of Glencoe, 1957.

Simon, Herbert A.: *Administrative Behavior,* 2d ed., New York: The Macmillan Company, 1957a.

————: *Models of Man, Social and Rational,* New York: John Wiley & Sons, Inc., 1957b.

————: "On the Concept of Organizational Goal," *Administrative Science Quarterly,* vol. 9, June, 1964, pp. 1–22.

————: *The New Science of Management Decision,* New York: Harper & Row, Publishers, Incorporated, 1960.

————, Harold Guetzkow, George Kozmetsky, and Gordon Tyndall: *Centralization vs. Decentralization in Organizing the Controller's Department,* New York: Controllership Foundation, 1954.

Stanton, Alfred H., and Morris S. Schwartz: *The Mental Hospital,* New York: Basic Books, Inc., Publishers, 1954.

Starbuck, William H.: "Organizational Growth and Development," in

James G. March (ed.), *Handbook of Organizations,* Chicago: Rand McNally & Company, 1965.

Stinchcombe, Arthur L.: "Bureaucratic and Craft Administration of Production: A Comparative Study," *Administrative Science Quarterly,* vol. 4, September, 1959, pp. 168–187.

————: "Social Structure and Organizations," in James G. March (ed.), *Handbook of Organizations,* Chicago: Rand McNally & Company, 1965.

Stouffer, Samuel A. et al.: *The American Soldier,* Princeton, N.J.: Princeton University Press, 1949. Vol. 1, "Adjustment During Army Life"; and vol. 2, "Combat and Its Aftermath."

————: *The American Soldier,* Princeton, N.J.: Princeton University Press, 1950. Vol. 4, "Measurement and Prediction."

Strauss, George: "Tactics of Lateral Relationship: The Purchasing Agent," *Administrative Science Quarterly,* vol. 7, September, 1962, pp. 161–186.

Stryker, Sheldon: "The Collegial Organization: Some Dysfunctional Elements," working paper for Seminar in the Social Science of Organizations, Pittsburgh, June, 1963 (mimeo).

Sykes, Gresham M.: "The Corruption of Authority and Rehabilitation," *Social Forces,* vol. 34, March, 1956, pp. 257–262.

Taylor, Frederick W.: *Scientific Management,* New York: Harper & Row, Publishers, Incorporated, 1911.

Thibaut, John W., and Harold H. Kelley: *The Social Psychology of Groups,* New York: John Wiley & Sons, Inc., 1959.

Thomas, Edwin J.: "Role Conceptions and Organizational Size," *American Sociological Review,* vol. 24, February, 1959, pp. 30–37.

Thompson, James D.: "Authority and Power in 'Identical' Organizations," *American Journal of Sociology,* vol. 62, November, 1956, pp. 290–301.

————: "Common and Uncommon Elements in Administration," in *The Social Welfare Forum, 1962,* New York: Columbia University Press, 1962a.

————: "Decision-making, The Firm, and the Market," in W. W. Cooper et al. (eds.), *New Perspectives in Organization Research,* New York: John Wiley & Sons, Inc., 1964.

————: *The Organization of Executive Action,* Technical Report No. 12,

Air Force Base Project, Chapel Hill, N.C.: Institute for Research in Social Science, University of North Carolina, 1953 (mimeo).

————: "Organizational Management of Conflict," *Administrative Science Quarterly*, vol. 4, March, 1960, pp. 389–409.

————: "Organizations and Output Transactions," *American Journal of Sociology*, vol. 68, November, 1962b, pp. 309–324.

———— and Frederick L. Bates: "Technology, Organization, and Administration," *Administrative Science Quarterly*, vol. 2, December, 1957, pp. 325–342.

———— and Robert W. Hawkes: "Disaster, Community Organization, and Administrative Process," in George W. Baker and Dwight W. Chapman (eds.), *Man and Society in Disaster*, New York: Basic Books, Inc., Publishers, 1962.

———— and William J. McEwen: "Organizational Goals and Environment: Goal-setting as an Interaction Process," *American Sociological Review*, vol. 23, February, 1958, pp. 23–31.

———— and Arthur Tuden: "Strategies, Structures and Processes of Organizational Decision," in James D. Thompson et al. (eds.), *Comparative Studies in Administration*, Pittsburgh, Pa.: The University of Pittsburgh Press, 1959.

Trist, E. L., and K. W. Bamforth: "Social and Psychological Consequences of the Longwall Method of Coal-Getting," *Human Relations*, vol. 4, February, 1951, pp. 3–38.

von Neumann, J., and O. Morgenstern: *Theory of Games and Economic Behavior*, Princeton, N.J.: Princeton University Press, 1944.

Weber, Max: *The Theory of Social and Economic Organization*, A. M. Henderson and Talcott Parsons (trans.), and Talcott Parsons (ed.), New York: The Free Press of Glencoe, 1947.

Whisler, Thomas L.: "The 'Assistant-to' in Four Administrative Settings," *Administrative Science Quarterly*, vol. 5, September, 1960, pp. 181–217.

————: "Measuring Centralization of Control in Business Organizations," in W. W. Cooper et al. (eds.), *New Perspectives in Organization Research*, New York: John Wiley & Sons, Inc., 1964.

White, Harrison: "Management Conflict and Sociometric Structure," *American Journal of Sociology*, vol. 67, September, 1961, pp. 185–199.

Wilson, James Q.: "Innovation in Organization: Notes toward a Theory," in James D. Thompson (ed.), *Approaches to Organizational Design,* Pittsburgh, Pa.: The University of Pittsburgh Press, 1966.

Woodward, Joan: *Industrial Organization: Theory and Practice,* London: Oxford University Press, 1965.

Zald, Mayer N.: "Power and Conflict in Correctional Institutions," *Administrative Science Quarterly,* vol. 7, June, 1962, pp. 22–49.

——— and Patricia Denton: "From Evangelism to General Service: The Transformation of the YMCA," *Administrative Science Quarterly,* vol. 8, September, 1963, pp. 214–234.

name index

Abegglen, James C., 103
Anderson, Theodore R., 74
Argyris, Chris, 22, 79, 96, 107
Ashby, W. Ross, 4
Atkinson, John W., 118
Avery, Robert W., 105

Bamforth, K. W., 51
Barnard, Chester I., 7, 8, 60, 105, 106, 148
Bartlett, Sir Frederic, 4
Bates, Frederick L., xxvii, 15n
Baumol, W. J., 83
Beck, Carl, xxviii
Becker, Howard S., 107
Belknap, Ivan, 23, 67
Berelson, Bernard, xxvi
Berliner, Joseph S., 29
Bidwell, Charles E., 43
Blau, Peter M., 23, 71, 96, 107, 112, 119, 120

Boland, Margaret, 74
Boland, Walter, 74
Boulding, Kenneth E., 44, 60, 154

Callahan, Raymond E., 91
Caplow, Theodore, 91, 139
Carlson, Richard O., xxvii, 79, 105
Carlson, Sune, 30
Cassell, Frank H., 103
Chandler, Alfred D., Jr., 41, 42, 46, 47, 49, 70, 74–77, 80, 119, 154
Clark, Burton R., 7, 31, 126, 157
Cloward, Richard A., 80
Cohen, Albert K., 122
Coleman, James S., 69
Costello, Timothy W., 106
Cottrell, W. Fred, 154
Cressy, Donald R., 137
Crozier, Michel, 10, 129
Cyert, Richard M., 8–10, 12, 34, 83, 97, 120, 126–128, 132, 151

subject index

CPSIA information can be obtained at www.ICGtesting.com
Printed in the USA
BVOW02s1454260813

329394BV00002B/9/P